Scaling Success with MTSS

A Guide to Effective MTSS Professional Development

ANTHONY J FITZPATRICK ED.D.

Copyright © 2025 MTSS Leadership Network

All rights reserved.

No part of this book may be reproduced or transmitted in any form or by any means, electronic or mechanical, including photocopying, recording, or by any information storage and retrieval system, without permission in writing from the publisher.

ISBN-13: **978-0-9864377-6-2**
Published in the United States of America
MTSS Leadership Network

About the Author

Anthony J. Fitzpatrick, Ed.D. is a distinguished educational leader, author, and scholar with a passion for transforming education through data-driven decision-making, equitable instructional practices, and Multi-Tiered Systems of Support (MTSS). With over two decades of experience in education, Dr. Fitzpatrick has served in various roles, including Assistant Superintendent for Curriculum and Instruction, principal, supervisor, and instructional leader. His expertise spans professional development, instructional leadership, and strategic implementation of educational frameworks that foster student success.

Dr. Fitzpatrick holds a Doctor of Education in Instructional Leadership from the American College of Education, a Master of Education in School Leadership, and a Bachelor of Arts in History with a concentration in International Studies from Rowan University. Throughout his career, he has been a driving force behind initiatives that prioritize achievement, equity, innovation, and sustainable educational change.

As an Associate Professor of Education at the University of Phoenix, Dr. Fitzpatrick mentors doctoral students, teaching courses in educational leadership, curriculum development, and technology integration. He is also an accomplished grant writer, securing competitive funding to expand access to high-quality education programs.

Dr. Fitzpatrick is the author of several influential books on MTSS, including:

- **Blueprint for Success: Implementing MTSS in Your School District** – A comprehensive guide for educators and administrators to develop, implement, and sustain an effective MTSS framework.

- **Sustaining Success with MTSS: Advanced Data Strategies for Transforming MTSS into a Lasting Framework for Excellence** – A deep dive into predictive analytics and data-driven strategies for ensuring long-term MTSS effectiveness.

Beyond his published works, Dr. Fitzpatrick has been a sought-after speaker and consultant, presenting at national and regional education conferences on topics such as school improvement, instructional leadership, and fostering inclusive learning environments. He has also played a key role in state and federal education initiatives, working with organizations such as the New Jersey Department of Education to develop innovative programs that enhance student learning outcomes.

Committed to shaping the future of education, Dr. Fitzpatrick continues to advocate for systems that support all learners, leveraging research-based practices to create sustainable, high-impact change in schools and districts nationwide.

Acknowledgments

A work of this magnitude is never the effort of one person alone. It is the result of collaboration, shared wisdom, and the unwavering support of many individuals who have contributed to my understanding of Multi-Tiered Systems of Support (MTSS) and professional development.

To My Colleagues & Mentors

I extend my deepest gratitude to my colleagues, fellow educators, and district leaders who have shared their experiences, insights, and best practices. Your commitment to refining MTSS implementation and supporting educators has been both inspiring and invaluable.

A special thank you to the instructional coaches, interventionists, and professional development leaders whose dedication ensures that teachers and students receive the resources they need to thrive. Your work in the field is the heart of sustainable, impactful education.

To My Support System

To my family and friends—thank you for your patience and encouragement throughout this journey. Writing this book required long hours, deep reflection, and countless revisions, and your unwavering belief in me kept me moving forward.

To the Educators and Leaders Who Will Use This Book

This book is a reflection of the collective work of countless professionals striving to improve student outcomes through effective, research-based professional learning. To the teachers, administrators, and MTSS practitioners who will apply these strategies in their schools—thank you for your dedication to transforming education through intentional, sustained professional development.

Final Gratitude

Finally, I am deeply grateful to the researchers, authors, and education thought leaders whose work has shaped the foundation of MTSS and evidence-based professional learning. Their contributions continue to guide and refine the way we support educators and improve student success.

It is my hope that this book serves as a practical, meaningful resource that helps you navigate, implement, and sustain effective MTSS professional development in ways that positively impact both educators and students for years to come.

With gratitude,
Anthony J. Fitzpatrick, EdD

Table of Contents

    About the Author 3

Acknowledgments **4**

  To My Colleagues & Mentors 4

  To My Support System 4

  To the Educators and Leaders Who Will Use This Book 4

  Final Gratitude 4

Chapter 1: Designing MTSS-Focused Professional Development **15**

  Section 1: Chapter Overview **15**

    Introduction to the Chapter's Focus 15

    Key Objectives and Learning Outcomes 15

  Section 2: Theoretical and Research-Based Foundations **17**

    Overview of Relevant Theories, Models, and Frameworks 17

    Summary of Recent Research Findings Related to MTSS Professional Development 20

    Connecting Theory to Practice 21

  Section 3: Best Practices and Implementation Strategies **21**

    Introduction 21

    Best Practices for MTSS Professional Development 21

    Strategies for Implementing MTSS Professional Development 22

    Conclusion 25

  Section 4: Common Challenges and Solutions **26**

    Introduction 26

    Common Challenges in MTSS Professional Development 26

    Solutions to Overcome MTSS Professional Development Challenges 28

    Conclusion 30

  Section 5: Assessing the Effectiveness of Professional Development **31**

    Introduction 31

    Key Metrics for Evaluating MTSS Professional Development 31

    Models for Evaluating MTSS Professional Development 32

    Methods for Collecting Data on PD Effectiveness 33

    Using Data for Continuous Improvement 34

    Conclusion 35

Chapter 2: Essential Training Modules for MTSS Practitioners **36**

Section 1: Chapter Overview 36
Introduction to the Chapter's Focus 36
Key Objectives and Learning Outcomes 36

Section 2: MTSS Foundations 38
Introduction 38
Key Learning Objectives..38
Historical Context and Legal Foundations 38
Understanding the Core Components of MTSS...............................39
Distinguishing MTSS from RTI and PBIS 42
The Role of Equity in MTSS..42
Conclusion 43

Section 3: Tiered Instruction and Intervention Strategies.......................... 43
Introduction 43
Key Learning Objectives..44
Overview of the Three-Tiered Framework 45

Tier 1: Universal Support (Core Instruction for All Students) 46
Key Characteristics of Tier 1..46
Best Practices for Tier 1 Instruction 46
Data Collection at Tier 1..46

Tier 2: Targeted Support (Some Students) 47
Key Characteristics of Tier 2..47
Best Practices for Tier 2 Instruction 47
Data Collection at Tier 2..47

Tier 3: Intensive Support (Few Students) 48
Key Characteristics of Tier 3..48
Best Practices for Tier 3 Instruction 48
Data Collection at Tier 3..48
Conclusion 49

Section 4: Data-Driven Decision-Making in MTSS.................................... 49
Introduction 49
Key Learning Objectives..50
The Role of Data in MTSS 50

Key Types of Data Collection in MTSS 51
1. Universal Screening: Identifying At-Risk Students......................51

2. Progress Monitoring: Tracking Student Growth..52

3. Diagnostic Assessments: Pinpointing Root Causes..52

Using Data to Drive Instructional Decisions..**53**

1. Data-Based Decision-Making Meetings 53

2. Differentiated Intervention Adjustments 53

3. Visualizing Data to Guide Conversations 54

Conclusion 54

Section 5: Collaboration and Team-Based Problem-Solving in MTSS **55**

Introduction 55

Key Learning Objectives...55

The Role of Collaboration in MTSS..55

Key MTSS Team Roles and Responsibilities 56

Structuring Effective MTSS Team Meetings 57

The MTSS Problem-Solving Process 58

Fostering Family and Community Partnerships in MTSS 59

Conclusion 59

Section 6: Culturally Responsive and Equity-Based MTSS Practices............**60**

Introduction 60

Key Learning Objectives...60

The Role of Equity in MTSS...60

Identifying Systemic Barriers in MTSS 61

Implementing Culturally Responsive Teaching and Intervention Strategies........62

Reducing Bias in MTSS Data Collection and Decision-Making..........................63

Promoting an Inclusive and Culturally Affirming School Climate 63

Conclusion 64

Section 7: Behavioral and Social-Emotional Supports in MTSS **64**

Introduction 64

Key Learning Objectives...65

Integrating PBIS, SEL, and Mental Health Support in MTSS.............................65

Tiered Behavioral and Social-Emotional Supports **66**

Tier 1: Universal Behavioral and SEL Supports (All Students) 66

Tier 2: Targeted Behavioral and SEL Supports (Some Students) 67

Tier 3: Intensive Behavioral and SEL Supports (Few Students) 68

    Using Data to Monitor Behavior and Social-Emotional Growth 68

    Conclusion 69

Chapter 3: Assessing the Effectiveness of MTSS Professional Development 70

Section 1: Chapter Overview 70

    Introduction to the Chapter's Focus 70

    Key Objectives and Learning Outcomes 70

Section 2: Theoretical Models for Evaluating Professional Development 72

    Introduction 72

    Key Learning Objectives 72

Guskey's Five Levels of Professional Development Evaluation (2000) 73

Kirkpatrick's Four Levels of Training Evaluation (1994) 74

Comparing Guskey's and Kirkpatrick's Models 75

Selecting the Right Evaluation Methods for MTSS PD 75

    Conclusion 76

Section 3: Key Performance Indicators (KPIs) for Evaluating MTSS Professional Development 77

    Introduction 77

    Key Learning Objectives 77

    Defining Key Performance Indicators (KPIs) in MTSS PD 78

Key Performance Indicators for MTSS Professional Development 78

    1. Educator Engagement & Participation Metrics 78

    2. Implementation Fidelity & Application Metrics 79

    3. Student Impact & Outcome Metrics 80

Using KPI Dashboards to Track MTSS PD Effectiveness 80

    Best Practices for KPI Dashboards 81

    Conclusion 81

Section 4: Feedback Collection and Continuous Improvement Strategies 82

    Introduction 82

    Key Learning Objectives 82

Collecting Meaningful Feedback on MTSS Professional Development 82

    Best Practices for Gathering Feedback 83

Methods for Collecting MTSS PD Feedback 84

Analyzing MTSS Professional Development Effectiveness 85

    Step-by-Step Process for PD Effectiveness Analysis 85

Continuous Improvement in MTSS Professional Development **86**

    The Continuous Improvement Cycle for MTSS PD 86

Encouraging Reflective Practice and Growth **87**

    Conclusion 87

Section 5: Case Studies of Successful MTSS Professional Development Programs 88

    Introduction 88

    Key Learning Objectives 88

Case Study 1: District-Wide MTSS Implementation with Coaching Support **88**

    Training Model: 89

    Results: 89

    Key Takeaways: 89

Case Study 2: Data-Driven MTSS Training for Rural Schools **89**

    Training Model: 90

    Results: 90

    Key Takeaways: 90

Case Study 3: Equity-Focused MTSS PD in an Urban District **90**

    Training Model: 91

    Results: 91

    Key Takeaways: 91

Common Themes and Best Practices from Case Studies **91**

    Conclusion 92

Chapter 4: Designing a District-Wide MTSS Professional Development Plan ... 93

    Section 1: Chapter Overview **93**

        Introduction to the Chapter's Focus 93

        Key Objectives and Learning Outcomes 93

    Section 2: Establishing Clear Goals and Alignment with District Priorities .. **95**

        Introduction 95

        Key Learning Objectives 95

    Defining MTSS Professional Development Goals **95**

        Characteristics of Strong MTSS PD Goals 96

        Aligning MTSS Professional Development with District Priorities 96

    Developing a District-Wide MTSS PD Vision Statement **97**

        Key Components of a Strong MTSS PD Vision Statement 97

Using Data to Inform MTSS PD Goal-Setting 98
Key Data Sources for Informing PD Goals 98
Conclusion 98
Section 3: Stakeholder Collaboration in MTSS PD Planning 99
Introduction 99
Key Learning Objectives 99
Key Stakeholders in MTSS PD Planning 99
Engaging Educators in MTSS PD Design 100
Why Teacher Input Matters 100
Best Practices for Teacher Engagement 101
The Role of Administrators in MTSS PD Implementation 101
How Administrators Can Support MTSS PD 101
Engaging Families & Community Partners in MTSS Training 102
Best Practices for Family & Community Engagement 102
Creating Sustainable Collaborative Structures for MTSS PD 102
Best Practices for Sustaining MTSS PD Collaboration 102
Conclusion 103
Section 4: Developing a Structured, Multi-Phase MTSS PD Timeline 104
Introduction 104
Key Learning Objectives 104
The Importance of a Multi-Phase PD Approach 104
Problems with One-Time Training Sessions 105
Benefits of a Multi-Phase PD Model 105
Structuring a Year-Long MTSS PD Timeline 105
Figure 4.2: Multi-Phase MTSS PD Timeline 106
Phase 1: Foundational Training (Summer & Early Fall) 106
Goal: Build educator knowledge of MTSS principles, tiered interventions, and data-driven decision-making. 106
Key Activities: 106
Phase 2: Initial Implementation & Coaching (Fall & Winter) 107
Goal: Support educators as they begin implementing MTSS strategies, ensuring fidelity and confidence in application. 107
Key Activities: 107
Phase 3: Advanced Skill Development (Winter & Spring) 107

- Goal: Deepen educators' ability to use data-driven decision-making and equity-focused MTSS practices.. 107
- Key Activities: 107

Phase 4: Evaluation & Continuous Improvement (Spring & Summer) **108**
- Goal: Assess the impact of MTSS PD, refine training content, and plan for the next year. 108
- Key Activities: 108
- Conclusion 108

Section 5: Effective Resource and Funding Allocation for MTSS PD **109**
- Introduction 109
- Key Learning Objectives 109

Key Resources Needed for Effective MTSS PD **110**

Funding Sources for MTSS Professional Development **111**
- Table 4.2: Key Funding Sources for MTSS PD 111

Allocating Resources Effectively **112**
- Best Practices for Resource Allocation 112

Leveraging Grants, Partnerships, and Cost-Effective Strategies **112**
- 1. Applying for Federal & State Grants 112
- 2. Partnering with Universities & Educational Organizations 113
- 3. Using Cost-Effective PD Models 113

Developing a District-Wide MTSS PD Budget Plan **114**
- Key Components of an MTSS PD Budget Plan 114
- Conclusion 114

Section 6: Monitoring and Sustaining MTSS Professional Development Efforts **115**
- Introduction 115
- Key Learning Objectives 115

Monitoring the Effectiveness of MTSS Professional Development **115**
- Why Monitoring Matters 115

Key Metrics for MTSS PD Monitoring **116**
- Table 4.3: Key MTSS PD Monitoring Metrics 116

Using Data to Refine and Improve MTSS PD **117**
- Best Practices for Using MTSS PD Data 117

Sustaining Professional Learning Over Time **117**
- 1. Embedding Coaching & Mentorship 117
- 2. Leveraging Professional Learning Communities (PLCs) 118

- 3. Building Leadership Support & Accountability 118
  - How Administrators Can Support MTSS PD Sustainability 118
- **Developing a Long-Term MTSS PD Sustainability Plan** **119**
  - Key Components of an MTSS PD Sustainability Plan 119
  - Conclusion 119

Chapter 5: Case Study – Implementing a Sustainable, High-Impact MTSS Professional Development Model 120

Section 1: Chapter Overview 120
- Introduction to the Chapter's Focus 120
- Key Objectives and Learning Outcomes 120
- District Profile and Context 121
- Key Phases of Implementation 121
- Key Challenges and Solutions 123
- Best Practices from the Case Study 124
- Lessons Learned 124
- Conclusion 125

Section 2: Practical Guidelines for Replicating the Model in Other Districts 125
- Introduction 125
- Key Learning Objectives 126

Step 1: Conduct a Readiness Assessment 126
- Key Readiness Indicators 126

Step 2: Develop a Phased MTSS PD Implementation Plan 126
- Table 5.1: Recommended Phases for Implementing MTSS PD 127

Step 3: Assign MTSS Leadership Roles & Responsibilities 127
- Table 5.2: MTSS PD Leadership Roles 127

Step 4: Embed Coaching & Collaborative Learning Structures 128
- Best Practices for Sustaining MTSS Learning 128

Step 5: Create an MTSS PD Tracking & Accountability System 128
- Table 5.3: MTSS PD Data Collection Methods 129

Step 6: Sustain MTSS PD Through Long-Term Planning 129
- Strategies for Long-Term MTSS PD Success 129
- Conclusion 130

Section 3: Customizable Templates and Planning Tools for MTSS PD Implementation 130

Introduction 130
Key Learning Objectives 131

Essential MTSS PD Planning Templates and Tools 131

1. MTSS Professional Development Planning Template 131
2. MTSS Training Roadmap Template 132
3. MTSS Coaching & Support Schedule Template 133
4. MTSS Implementation Fidelity Checklist 134
5. MTSS PD Evaluation & Feedback Form 135

How to Use These Templates for Maximum Impact 135

Best Practices for Implementing MTSS PD Planning Tools 135
Conclusion 136

Chapter 6: Final Recommendations for Ensuring District-Wide MTSS PD Success 137

Section 1: Chapter Overview 137

Introduction to the Chapter's Focus 137
Key Objectives and Learning Outcomes 137

Final Best Practices for Successful MTSS Professional Development 138

1. Align Training with District Priorities and Student Needs 138
2. Implement a Phased, Scalable Approach to Professional Development 138
3. Embed Ongoing Coaching and Collaborative Learning Structures 139
4. Use Data to Track PD Impact and Adjust Training Strategies 139
5. Ensure Leadership Commitment and Long-Term Sustainability 140

Common Pitfalls to Avoid in MTSS PD Implementation 140

Table 6.2: Common Challenges and Solutions in MTSS Training 140

District-Wide Action Plan for MTSS Professional Development 141

Conclusion 141

Section 2: Closing Remarks and Call to Action 142

Introduction 142
Key Takeaways from the Book 142

Next Steps for District Leaders and Educators 143

1. Conduct a District-Wide MTSS PD Audit 143
2. Establish a Long-Term MTSS PD Vision and Sustainability Plan 143
Key Elements of an MTSS PD Sustainability Plan 143
3. Foster a Culture of Continuous Improvement and Innovation 144

A Call to Action: Committing to Effective and Sustainable MTSS Professional Development 145
A Message to District Leaders: 145
A Message to Educators: 145
A Message to Stakeholders and Policymakers: 145
Final Words: The Path Forward 146
Glossary of Key Terms 147
Conclusion 151
Scholarly References 152
Multi-Tiered System of Supports (MTSS) & Intervention Effectiveness 152
Professional Development & Educator Capacity Building 152
Coaching & Job-Embedded Professional Learning 153
Data-Driven Decision Making & MTSS Fidelity Monitoring 153
Equity and Culturally Responsive MTSS Practices 154
Sustaining MTSS Professional Development & Scaling Impact 154
Conclusion 155
Additional Scholarly References 156
Specialized References for MTSS Professional Development 156
Behavioral Interventions & Social-Emotional Learning (SEL) in MTSS 156
1. Positive Behavioral Interventions and Supports (PBIS) and MTSS 156
2. Social-Emotional Learning (SEL) and Trauma-Informed MTSS 156
Technology-Enhanced Professional Development (PD) for MTSS 157
3. Online and Hybrid Learning Models for Educator PD 157
4. Virtual Coaching and Data Systems for MTSS 157
MTSS and Special Education 158
5. MTSS for Students with Disabilities and Inclusive Practices 158
6. Equity-Focused Special Education and MTSS 158
Conclusion 159

Chapter 1: Designing MTSS-Focused Professional Development

Section 1: Chapter Overview

Introduction to the Chapter's Focus

The success of a Multi-Tiered System of Supports (MTSS) hinges on the knowledge, skills, and ongoing development of the practitioners implementing it. MTSS is a dynamic framework that requires educators to adapt and refine their approaches to intervention, data analysis, and collaboration. Without well-structured professional development (PD), even the most well-intended MTSS initiatives can fail due to inconsistent implementation, gaps in understanding, and a lack of coherence across teams.

This chapter explores the foundational elements of designing effective professional development for MTSS practitioners. It delves into the unique characteristics of MTSS-focused training, the essential components of a robust PD program, and the challenges and opportunities associated with professional learning in this space. By the end of the chapter, readers will gain insight into best practices for structuring and delivering high-impact MTSS training that supports educators in applying evidence-based interventions with fidelity.

Key Objectives and Learning Outcomes

This chapter provides an overview of the essential components of MTSS-focused professional development. Specifically, readers will:

- **Understand the importance of professional development in MTSS implementation** and how it differs from traditional teacher training.
- **Identify the key elements of effective MTSS professional development,** including needs assessments, job-embedded learning, and collaborative problem-solving.
- **Recognize common challenges in MTSS training** and explore strategies for overcoming them.
- **Examine real-world applications of MTSS PD** and how schools can create sustainable learning experiences for practitioners.
- **Develop an initial framework for structuring MTSS professional learning experiences,** ensuring alignment with research-based best practices.

To provide a visual representation of the interconnected elements of effective MTSS professional development, Figure 1.1 presents a model of the core components essential for building a sustainable training program.

Figure 1.1: Essential Components of MTSS Professional Development

Each of these components plays a critical role in ensuring that MTSS professional development is not only informative but also transformative, equipping educators with the skills and confidence to implement MTSS effectively in their schools. The next section of this chapter will explore why specialized professional development is essential for MTSS practitioners and how it differs from traditional teacher PD models.

Section 2: Theoretical and Research-Based Foundations

Overview of Relevant Theories, Models, and Frameworks

Effective professional development for Multi-Tiered System of Supports (MTSS) practitioners is rooted in established educational theories, adult learning models, and implementation science frameworks. To design meaningful and impactful training experiences, it is essential to understand how educators learn, how organizations implement change, and how tiered systems of support function in practice. This section explores the theoretical foundations that inform high-quality MTSS professional development.

Adult Learning Theory (Knowles, 1984)

Malcolm Knowles' **Adult Learning Theory** (Andragogy) emphasizes that adults learn differently than children. MTSS professional development should be designed around the following key principles of adult learning:

- **Self-Directed Learning:** MTSS practitioners must be given opportunities to take ownership of their professional learning experiences. Providing autonomy in PD allows educators to explore strategies that align with their instructional needs.
- **Experiential Learning:** Adults learn best through hands-on activities, case studies, and application-based learning. MTSS PD should incorporate real-world scenarios and problem-solving exercises.
- **Relevance to Practice:** Professional development must be directly applicable to the educator's role. Training should focus on real-life MTSS implementation rather than abstract theories.
- **Collaborative and Reflective Practice:** Learning should involve discussion, collaboration, and reflection to help practitioners integrate new knowledge into their daily routines

Implementation Science and the Active Implementation Framework (Fixsen et al., 2005)

MTSS professional development is not just about individual learning—it requires systemic implementation at the school and district levels. The Active Implementation Framework (AIF) provides a research-based model for ensuring that professional development translates into sustainable practice. The AIF consists of the following key elements:

- **Competency Drivers:** Training, coaching, and ongoing professional learning ensure that MTSS practitioners develop the necessary skills.
- **Organization Drivers:** School and district leadership must support the infrastructure needed for sustained MTSS implementation, including time for training and collaboration.
- **Leadership Drivers:** Effective MTSS implementation requires leaders who can address challenges and provide strategic guidance for continuous improvement.

Figure 1.2 provides a visual representation of how these elements interact within MTSS professional development.

Figure 1.2: Active Implementation Framework for MTSS Professional Development

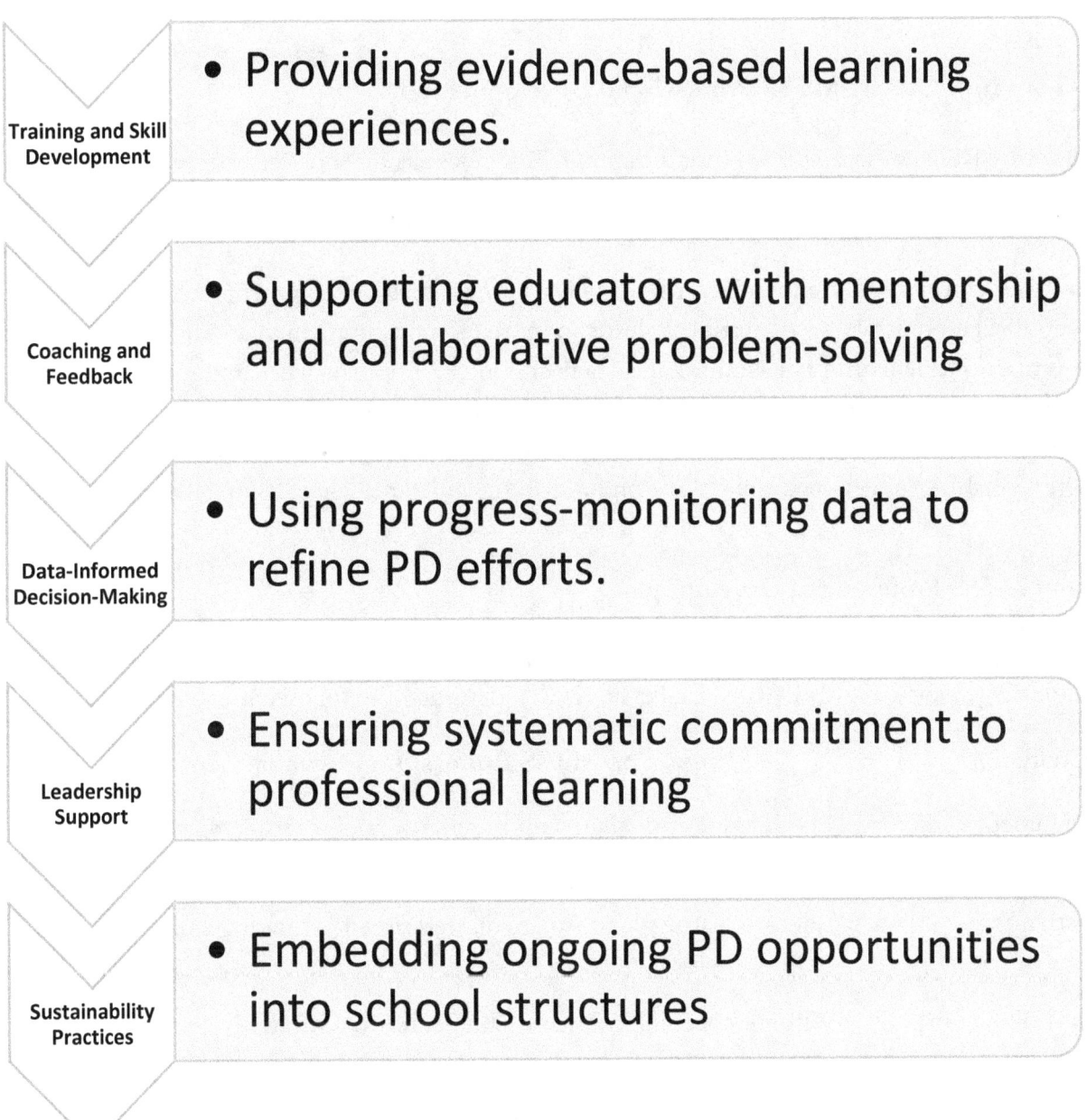

By incorporating the principles of adult learning theory and the Active Implementation Framework, professional development for MTSS practitioners can become more effective and sustainable.

Summary of Recent Research Findings Related to MTSS Professional Development

Research on professional development within MTSS frameworks underscores the need for structured, ongoing, and data-driven training. Recent studies highlight several best practices and challenges in this area.

The Impact of High-Quality MTSS Professional Development

A meta-analysis by Kennedy et al. (2018) found that MTSS-focused PD is most effective when it includes ongoing coaching and real-time application. The study emphasized that:

- **One-time workshops are insufficient.** Sustained professional development, including follow-up support and practice-based feedback, leads to more effective implementation.
- **Job-embedded learning is essential.** Teachers and interventionists who engage in PD that is integrated into their daily work report higher confidence and skill retention.
- **Collaborative learning communities enhance implementation.** Schools that establish PLCs (Professional Learning Communities) around MTSS see greater fidelity in implementation.

Challenges in MTSS Professional Development

Despite the benefits, research also points to common barriers in designing and delivering MTSS professional development. A study by Brownell et al. (2021) identified the following obstacles:

Challenge	Impact on MTSS Professional Development
Lack of Alignment with School Goals	PD that does not align with broader school improvement efforts loses effectiveness.
Time Constraints	Educators struggle to find dedicated time for training amid daily responsibilities.
Insufficient Follow-Up Support	Without coaching or mentorship, educators often revert to previous practices.
Variability in MTSS Knowledge	Professional development must account for differences in educators' prior MTSS experience.

Addressing these challenges requires designing PD that is systemic, ongoing, and embedded within daily practice.

Connecting Theory to Practice

By grounding professional development in adult learning theory and implementation science, schools can create more effective and sustainable learning experiences for MTSS practitioners. Research underscores that ongoing coaching, collaboration, and job-embedded training are essential for ensuring that educators can successfully implement tiered interventions with fidelity.

In the next section, we will explore best practices for structuring professional development that aligns with these theoretical foundations and research-based findings.

Section 3: Best Practices and Implementation Strategies

Introduction

Designing effective professional development (PD) for Multi-Tiered System of Supports (MTSS) practitioners requires a strategic approach that aligns with research-based best practices. Successful MTSS implementation depends on educators' ability to collect and analyze data, differentiate instruction, and collaborate effectively within an interdisciplinary framework. However, traditional PD models—such as one-size-fits-all workshops or isolated training sessions—often fail to provide the depth and support necessary for long-term success.

This section outlines best practices and implementation strategies for designing meaningful and sustainable MTSS professional learning experiences. These strategies focus on structured learning pathways, job-embedded coaching, collaborative problem-solving, and continuous assessment to ensure that professional development leads to improved student outcomes.

Best Practices for MTSS Professional Development

Effective MTSS professional development programs share several core characteristics. Research and practical application suggest that high-quality PD should be:

1. **Job-Embedded and Application-Based**
    - PD should be integrated into educators' daily responsibilities rather than treated as an isolated event.

- Hands-on learning opportunities, such as case studies, classroom simulations, and data-driven decision-making exercises, help bridge the gap between theory and practice.

2. **Ongoing and Sustained**

    - One-time workshops are ineffective for developing long-term competencies.
    - A structured PD model should include follow-up sessions, coaching, and check-ins to ensure continuous growth.

3. **Collaborative and Multi-Disciplinary**

    - MTSS requires teamwork across multiple roles, including general educators, special educators, counselors, and administrators.
    - Professional development should encourage cross-disciplinary learning communities that foster problem-solving and shared responsibility.

4. **Data-Driven and Differentiated**

    - Just as MTSS tailors interventions to students' needs, PD should be personalized for educators based on their prior knowledge, experiences, and specific areas for growth.
    - Educators should use real student data in training exercises to strengthen their ability to apply MTSS principles in authentic contexts.

5. **Leadership-Supported and Culturally Responsive**

    - School and district leadership should actively participate in and support professional learning efforts.
    - Training should emphasize equity and culturally responsive practices to ensure that MTSS interventions meet the diverse needs of all students.

These core best practices serve as the foundation for the implementation strategies discussed in the following section.

Strategies for Implementing MTSS Professional Development

To ensure MTSS training is effective, schools and districts should adopt an intentional, structured approach that prioritizes continuous learning and accountability. The following strategies have been proven to enhance the effectiveness of MTSS professional development:

1. Establishing Structured Learning Pathways

Rather than providing disconnected training sessions, districts should develop multi-tiered learning pathways that align with educators' roles and responsibilities. These pathways should follow a progression model, moving from foundational knowledge to advanced application.

Table 1.3: MTSS Professional Development Learning Pathway

Stage	Focus Area	Implementation Strategy
Foundational Training	Overview of MTSS framework and tiered supports	Workshops, online modules
Skill Development	Data-driven decision-making, intervention strategies	Case studies, guided practice
Application & Coaching	Hands-on implementation, feedback loops	Coaching, peer observations
Sustainability & Leadership	Long-term MTSS integration, leadership roles	Learning communities, mentorship

A well-structured learning pathway ensures that all educators receive the necessary training at the right time and in the right context for their professional growth.

---

2. Incorporating Job-Embedded Coaching and Feedback

Research consistently highlights ongoing coaching as one of the most effective professional learning models (Kennedy et al., 2018). Schools should adopt instructional coaching frameworks that provide real-time support, allowing MTSS practitioners to receive feedback while actively implementing strategies.

Key components of effective coaching include:

- **Observational Learning:** Coaches and educators participate in classroom walk-throughs to analyze MTSS implementation.
- **Reflective Practice:** Educators engage in structured debriefs to discuss challenges and refine their interventions.
- **Peer Mentoring:** Veteran educators mentor newer MTSS practitioners, ensuring knowledge transfer.

A successful coaching model creates a culture of continuous learning, where educators feel **supported rather than evaluated** in their professional growth.

---

3. Creating Collaborative Learning Communities

MTSS is inherently **collaborative**, requiring input from general educators, interventionists, administrators, and student support teams. Schools should establish **Professional Learning Communities (PLCs)** that provide structured opportunities for cross-disciplinary teams to engage in shared problem-solving.

Best Practices for MTSS Learning Communities:

- ✓ Regularly scheduled PLC meetings focused on **real student data** Structured protocols for **problem-solving and case studies**
- ✓ Leadership participation to align PD with **school-wide goals**
- ✓ Digital collaboration spaces for ongoing **resource sharing**

By embedding collaboration into the fabric of professional development, schools ensure that MTSS remains a team-based, systemic approach rather than an isolated initiative.

---

4. Using Data to Drive Professional Development Decisions

MTSS emphasizes data-driven decision-making, and PD should reflect the same commitment to using evidence to guide instruction and intervention strategies. Professional development should include:

- **Training on data literacy** to help educators analyze progress-monitoring reports and intervention outcomes.
- **Real-time data applications**, where educators work with live student data during PD sessions.
- **Personalized PD plans** based on school and district MTSS implementation data, ensuring that training is relevant and responsive.

Figure 1.3 below illustrates how data is integrated into the MTSS professional development cycle.

Figure 1.3: The MTSS Professional Development Data Cycle

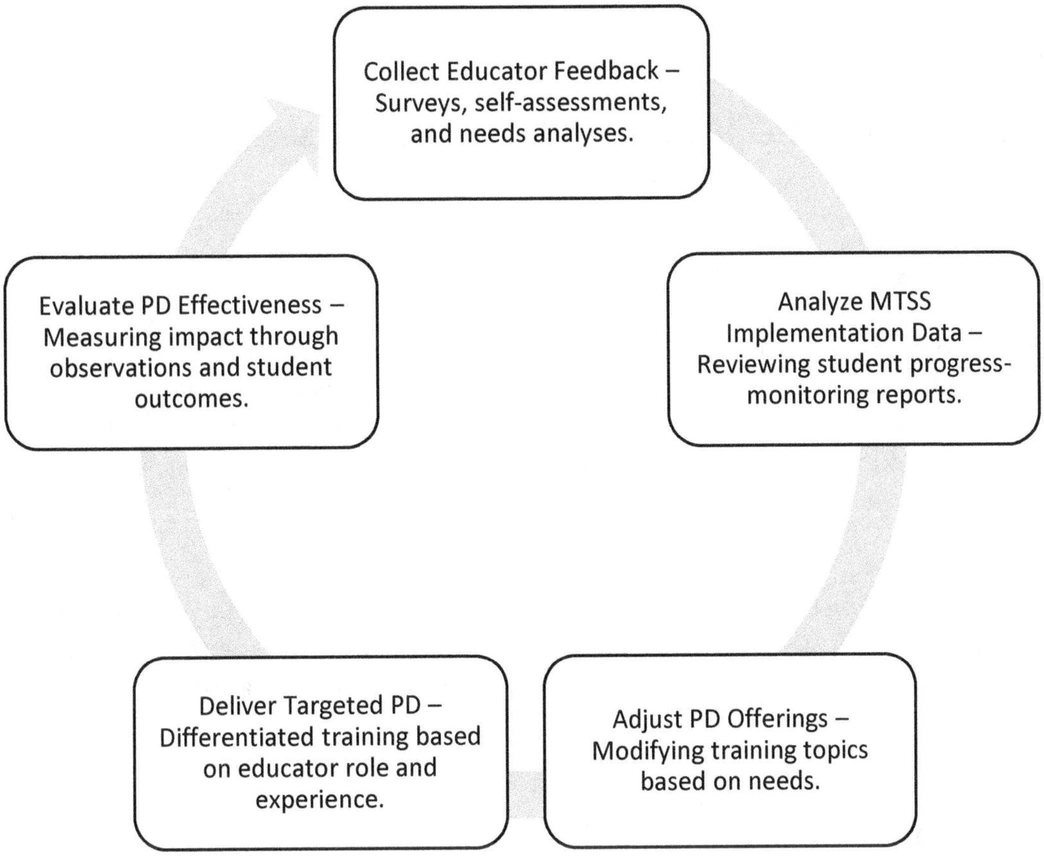

The cycle consists of five stages:
- Collect Educator Feedback – Surveys, self-assessments, and needs analyses.
- Analyze MTSS Implementation Data – Reviewing student progress-monitoring reports.
- Adjust PD Offerings – Modifying training topics based on needs.
- Deliver Targeted PD – Differentiated training based on educator role and experience.
- Evaluate PD Effectiveness – Measuring impact through observations and student outcomes.

By consistently using data to inform, refine, and personalize professional learning, schools can ensure that MTSS professional development is relevant, effective, and continuously improving.

Conclusion

Designing professional development for MTSS practitioners requires more than traditional training sessions. It demands a structured, data-driven, and job-embedded approach that supports educators at every stage of implementation. Best practices in MTSS professional development include:

- ✓ Establishing **structured learning pathways** aligned with educator roles
- ✓ Providing **ongoing coaching and feedback** to reinforce learning
- ✓ Encouraging **collaborative problem-solving** through learning communities
- ✓ Embedding **data-driven decision-making** into all professional learning efforts

By integrating these strategies, schools and districts can create a sustainable professional learning framework that empowers educators and improves MTSS outcomes. The next section will explore common challenges in MTSS professional development and practical solutions for overcoming them.

Section 4: Common Challenges and Solutions

Introduction

While professional development (PD) for Multi-Tiered System of Supports (MTSS) practitioners is essential for effective implementation, it is not without challenges. Schools and districts often struggle with issues such as time constraints, inconsistent implementation, limited resources, and varying levels of MTSS knowledge among educators. These challenges can undermine the effectiveness of PD and hinder MTSS fidelity.

This section explores common obstacles to designing and implementing high-quality MTSS professional development. More importantly, it provides research-based solutions to overcome these challenges, ensuring that professional learning efforts lead to sustained improvements in practice.

Common Challenges in MTSS Professional Development

Despite the best intentions, schools frequently encounter barriers that prevent MTSS training from being as effective as intended. These challenges fall into five primary categories:

1. Time Constraints and Scheduling Conflicts

One of the most significant barriers to professional development is finding time within the school schedule. Teachers, interventionists, and administrators are often overwhelmed with instructional responsibilities, meetings, and administrative duties, leaving little time for in-depth PD.

2. Inconsistent Implementation Across Schools and Teams

Even when PD is provided, implementation often varies across teachers, grade levels, and school sites. Some educators fully embrace MTSS, while others may struggle due to lack of clarity or confidence.

3. Limited Resources and Support Structures

Many schools face budgetary constraints that limit access to high-quality MTSS training, coaching, and materials. Without sufficient funding, PD can become inconsistent or reliant on self-directed learning, which may not be as effective.

4. Variability in Educator Knowledge and Experience

Educators come into MTSS professional development with varying levels of knowledge and expertise. Some may be well-versed in tiered intervention strategies, while others are completely new to the framework, making it difficult to design PD that meets everyone's needs.

5. Lack of Ongoing Coaching and Follow-Up

A one-time training session does not translate into long-term success. Research consistently shows that without **ongoing coaching and follow-up support**, most educators revert to previous practices rather than fully integrating new learning.

The following table summarizes these challenges and their impact on MTSS professional development.

Table 1.4: Common Challenges in MTSS Professional Development

Challenge	Impact on MTSS PD
Time Constraints	Educators struggle to participate in PD due to packed schedules.
Inconsistent Implementation	MTSS is applied differently across classrooms and schools.
Limited Resources	Schools lack funding for high-quality PD materials and coaching.
Variability in Educator Knowledge	Training does not meet the needs of all participants.
Lack of Ongoing Coaching	Educators revert to old habits without follow-up support.

Solutions to Overcome MTSS Professional Development Challenges

To ensure that professional learning effectively supports MTSS implementation, schools and districts must address these barriers with strategic, research-based solutions. The following approaches can help create more accessible, engaging, and sustainable professional development programs.

1. Embedding Professional Development Within the School Day

- ❖ **Solution:** Schools should **integrate PD into existing structures** rather than treating it as an add-on.

Implementation Strategies:

- Schedule **short, frequent learning sessions** (e.g., 20-30 minutes during staff meetings).
- Utilize **co-teaching and peer coaching** models to embed learning within daily practice.
- Implement **online learning modules** that educators can complete at their convenience.
- Incorporate **early release or late-start days** for PD without impacting instructional time.

- ❖ **Example in Practice:**
  A district in Illinois redesigned its professional development model by embedding weekly "MTSS Minutes" into faculty meetings, allowing staff to engage in bite-sized, focused training sessions rather than long workshops.

---

2. Standardizing Implementation with Clear Guidelines and Expectations

- ❖ **Solution:** Develop **clear implementation frameworks and accountability measures** to ensure consistency across classrooms and schools.

Implementation Strategies:

- Use **MTSS implementation rubrics** to guide and measure fidelity.
- Provide **tiered support templates** so educators can apply strategies with clarity.
- Offer **calibrated training sessions** to ensure all staff receive the same foundational knowledge.

- ❖ **Example in Practice:**
  A Florida district developed an MTSS Implementation Playbook, providing clear step-by-step guides for tiered interventions and data collection. This helped create consistency across all schools.

---

3. Leveraging Grants and Partnerships for Resources

- ❖ **Solution:** Schools should explore **alternative funding sources and strategic partnerships** to supplement professional development.

Implementation Strategies:

- Apply for **state and federal education grants** focused on intervention training.
- Partner with **universities and research organizations** to access training at a lower cost.
- Use **online, open-access PD platforms** to supplement in-person training.

- ❖ **Example in Practice:**
  A rural school district partnered with a local university to create an MTSS coaching program, where graduate students in education supported teachers with data collection and intervention strategies.

---

4. Differentiating PD Based on Educator Needs

- ❖ **Solution:** PD should be designed with **multiple entry points** based on educators' existing MTSS knowledge.

Implementation Strategies:

- Use **pre-assessments** to identify participants' baseline knowledge.
- Offer **tiered learning pathways** (beginner, intermediate, advanced) within PD sessions.
- Allow educators to **select PD topics** that align with their areas for growth.

- ❖ **Example in Practice:**
  A district in Texas launched a personalized MTSS PD model, where teachers could select self-paced courses based on their level of experience with MTSS interventions.

5. Implementing Coaching and Peer Support Networks

- ❖ **Solution:** Schools should prioritize **ongoing coaching, mentorship, and professional learning communities (PLCs)** to reinforce learning.

Implementation Strategies:

- Assign **MTSS coaches** who provide ongoing support through modeling and feedback.
- Create **peer observation programs**, where educators learn from one another.
- Establish **PLCs focused on MTSS problem-solving and data discussions**.

- ❖ **Example in Practice:**
  A middle school in New York established an MTSS Coaching Team, where instructional specialists rotated through classrooms to provide feedback, troubleshoot challenges, and reinforce best practices in tiered interventions.

Conclusion

While challenges in MTSS professional development are inevitable, strategic solutions can help overcome these barriers and create a culture of continuous learning and collaboration. Schools and districts can enhance MTSS professional development by:

- ✓ Embedding PD within the school day to address **time constraints**
- ✓ Standardizing implementation through **clear guidelines and expectations**
- ✓ Leveraging **grants and partnerships** to overcome **resource limitations**
- ✓ Differentiating PD to meet **the diverse needs of educators**
- ✓ Prioritizing **coaching and peer support** for sustained implementation

By applying these solutions, schools can increase the effectiveness and impact of professional development, ensuring that all educators have the skills and support needed to implement MTSS successfully.

The next section will explore assessment strategies for evaluating the effectiveness of MTSS professional development, ensuring that training efforts lead to measurable improvements in both educator practice and student outcomes.

Section 5: Assessing the Effectiveness of Professional Development

Introduction

Professional development (PD) is only as valuable as its impact. Schools and districts invest significant time and resources into training Multi-Tiered System of Supports (MTSS) practitioners, but without proper evaluation, it is difficult to determine whether the training leads to meaningful improvements in educator practice and student outcomes. Assessing the effectiveness of MTSS professional development is critical to ensuring that learning translates into action and that PD efforts result in sustained implementation.

This section explores key methods for evaluating MTSS PD, including quantitative and qualitative measures, feedback collection, and continuous improvement strategies. By using a combination of data sources, schools can refine their professional learning programs to better meet educators' needs and improve MTSS implementation fidelity.

Key Metrics for Evaluating MTSS Professional Development

A well-structured PD evaluation framework should assess the effectiveness of training at multiple levels, focusing on:

1. **Educator Engagement and Participation**
   - Are educators actively involved in training sessions?
   - Do they complete required PD activities and follow up with collaborative discussions?
2. **Knowledge Acquisition and Skill Development**
   - Do educators demonstrate an increased understanding of MTSS principles?
   - Can they effectively apply data-driven decision-making and intervention strategies?
3. **Implementation Fidelity**
   - Are educators applying the learned MTSS strategies correctly and consistently in their practice?
   - Are interventions being delivered as designed?
4. **Impact on Student Outcomes**

- Are MTSS-trained educators seeing measurable improvements in student progress?
- Do intervention effectiveness data align with professional learning goals?

Models for Evaluating MTSS Professional Development

Several established models provide structured approaches for evaluating professional learning programs. Two widely used models for PD assessment are Guskey's Five Levels of PD Evaluation and Kirkpatrick's Four Levels of Training Evaluation.

1. Guskey's Five Levels of Professional Development Evaluation (2000)

Guskey's framework provides a comprehensive approach to assessing PD effectiveness at different levels, from participant satisfaction to student achievement.

Table 1.5: Guskey's Five Levels of PD Evaluation Applied to MTSS

Level	Focus Area	MTSS Application
Level 1: Participant Reactions	Educator satisfaction with PD delivery	Post-training surveys, feedback forms
Level 2: Learning Outcomes	Knowledge and skills gained	Pre- and post-assessments, quizzes
Level 3: Organizational Support & Change	School/district support for PD	Leadership buy-in, alignment with school goals
Level 4: Educator Application	Implementation of new strategies	Classroom observations, coaching feedback
Level 5: Student Impact	Effects of PD on student achievement	Progress monitoring data, intervention outcomes

By assessing PD across these levels, schools can determine whether training efforts are leading to real changes in practice and student success.

2. Kirkpatrick's Four Levels of Training Evaluation (1994)

Similar to Guskey's model, Kirkpatrick's model evaluates PD effectiveness based on four progressive levels:

- **Level 1: Reaction** – Do participants find the training useful and engaging?
- **Level 2: Learning** – Have participants acquired new knowledge or skills?
- **Level 3: Behavior** – Are educators applying what they learned in real practice?
- **Level 4: Results** – Is there measurable improvement in student performance?

Schools can use this model to track progress over time, ensuring that PD translates into meaningful outcomes.

Methods for Collecting Data on PD Effectiveness

To accurately evaluate professional development, schools should use a combination of quantitative and qualitative methods. The following strategies provide multiple data points to assess MTSS PD.

1. Pre- and Post-Assessments

- ✓ Measure knowledge gains by testing educators before and after training sessions.
- ✓ Use surveys, quizzes, and case study analyses to assess learning retention.
- ❖ **Example:** A district uses a data-driven decision-making assessment before and after MTSS PD to measure improvement in educators' ability to analyze student progress data.

---

2. Educator Feedback and Surveys

- ✓ Collect participant feedback through post-training surveys and structured interviews.
- ✓ Use Likert-scale surveys to gauge confidence levels in applying MTSS strategies.
- ✓ Incorporate open-ended responses for qualitative insights.
- ❖ **Example:** A school administers a MTSS PD Satisfaction Survey, asking educators to rate the usefulness of training on a 1-5 scale and provide suggestions for improvement.

3. Classroom Observations and Fidelity Checks

- ✓ Conduct observations to ensure that **MTSS strategies are being implemented correctly**.
- ✓ Use **MTSS fidelity checklists** to assess intervention delivery.
- ✓ Provide coaching and feedback for **real-time improvement**.
- ❖ **Example:** A team of **MTSS coaches conducts monthly fidelity checks**, using a rubric to assess educators' application of data-driven interventions.

4. Student Performance Data Analysis

- ✓ Track student **progress-monitoring data** before and after PD implementation.
- ✓ Compare **intervention success rates** across MTSS-trained and non-MTSS-trained educators.
- ✓ Examine **achievement gaps** to see if targeted PD is improving student equity.
- ❖ **Example:** A district analyzes **universal screening scores** and finds that schools with structured MTSS PD have higher rates of student growth compared to schools without targeted training.

Using Data for Continuous Improvement

PD assessment should be an ongoing process, where schools continuously refine training efforts based on results. The following cycle, illustrated in Figure 1.4, demonstrates how schools can use PD evaluation data to make strategic improvements.

Figure 1.4: MTSS Professional Development Evaluation Cycle

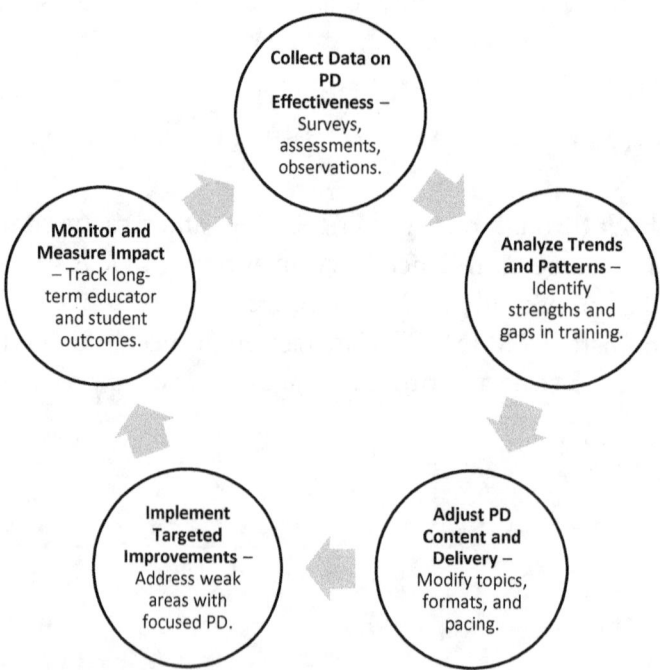

By continuously evaluating and refining PD, schools can ensure that professional learning remains relevant, effective, and aligned with MTSS goals.

Conclusion

Assessing MTSS professional development is essential for ensuring its success. By using structured evaluation models such as Guskey's Five Levels of PD Evaluation and Kirkpatrick's Four Levels of Training Evaluation, schools can track the effectiveness of training at multiple levels.

Key strategies for PD assessment include:

- ✓ **Pre- and post-assessments** to measure knowledge gains.
- ✓ **Educator surveys and feedback** to gauge engagement and usefulness.
- ✓ **Classroom observations and fidelity checks** to ensure proper implementation.
- ✓ **Student performance data analysis** to determine impact on learning.
- ✓ **Continuous improvement cycles** to refine PD efforts over time.

By implementing a data-driven approach to PD evaluation, schools can maximize the effectiveness of MTSS training, ensuring that educators receive the support they need to drive positive student outcomes.

The next chapter will explore essential training modules for MTSS practitioners, detailing the key content areas that should be included in professional learning programs.

Chapter 2: Essential Training Modules for MTSS Practitioners

Section 1: Chapter Overview

Introduction to the Chapter's Focus

Professional development for Multi-Tiered System of Supports (MTSS) practitioners must be structured, purposeful, and directly applicable to the challenges educators face in implementation. While Chapter 1 focused on designing and assessing professional development, this chapter explores the essential training modules that should be included in MTSS professional learning programs.

MTSS is a multi-dimensional framework that requires knowledge and skill development in tiered intervention strategies, data analysis, progress monitoring, collaboration, and culturally responsive practices. Without structured training modules covering these areas, educators may struggle to implement MTSS effectively and consistently.

In this chapter, we will examine the core topics that every MTSS training program should include, ensuring that practitioners receive the necessary foundation to apply MTSS principles with fidelity. Each module will include a discussion of key learning objectives, implementation strategies, and best practices for training delivery.

Key Objectives and Learning Outcomes

By the end of this chapter, readers will be able to:

- **Identify the essential training modules for MTSS professional development** and understand their importance in effective implementation.
- **Recognize the knowledge and skill components** required for successful MTSS practice.
- **Align training content with the needs of different educator roles,** including general educators, interventionists, special educators, and administrators.
- **Develop a structured training plan** that ensures comprehensive professional learning.
- **Apply best practices in delivering MTSS training modules,** ensuring that educators gain practical, job-embedded learning experiences.

To provide an overview of the critical training areas, Figure 2.1 presents a visual breakdown of the core MTSS training modules that will be discussed in this chapter.

Figure 2.1: Core MTSS Training Modules

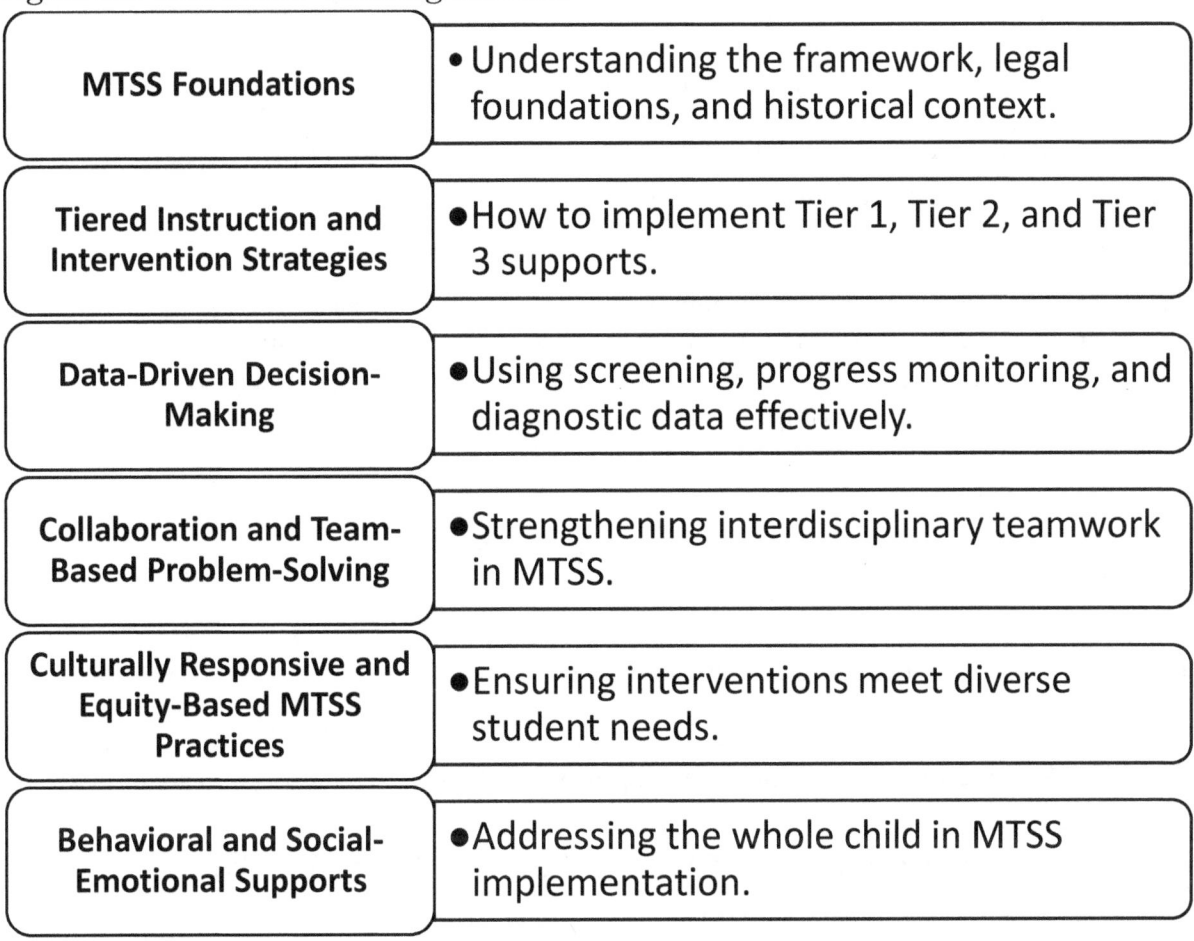

Each of these modules represents a critical area of knowledge and practice that MTSS practitioners must develop to ensure that MTSS is effectively implemented and sustained.

In the next section, we will begin with MTSS Foundations, covering the fundamental principles, historical development, and key components of a strong MTSS framework.

Section 2: MTSS Foundations

Introduction

Before educators can successfully implement a Multi-Tiered System of Supports (MTSS), they must first develop a strong foundational understanding of its principles, components, and goals. This foundational knowledge serves as the cornerstone of all other MTSS training and ensures that practitioners have a clear, consistent understanding of the framework's purpose and function.

This section provides an overview of the key elements of MTSS, including its historical development, legal foundations, and essential components. Additionally, it explores the distinctions between MTSS, Response to Intervention (RTI), and Positive Behavioral Interventions and Supports (PBIS) to help educators understand how these frameworks interact.

Key Learning Objectives

By the end of this training module, educators will be able to:

- **Define MTSS and explain its purpose** in supporting academic, behavioral, and social-emotional success.
- **Understand the historical evolution of MTSS** and its connection to federal and state educational policies.
- **Differentiate MTSS from RTI and PBIS** and understand how they function within a school system.
- **Identify the essential components of a strong MTSS framework** and the roles of various stakeholders.
- **Recognize the importance of MTSS in promoting equity** and ensuring that all students receive the support they need to succeed.

Historical Context and Legal Foundations

MTSS has evolved over several decades as a response to gaps in traditional educational models, particularly in identifying and supporting struggling students. Understanding the history and legal foundations of MTSS helps practitioners appreciate its significance and the policies that shape its implementation.

Key Milestones in the Development of MTSS

Year	Legislative or Educational Milestone	Impact on MTSS
1975	Education for All Handicapped Children Act (PL 94-142)	Required schools to provide **free and appropriate public education (FAPE)** to students with disabilities.
2001	No Child Left Behind Act (NCLB)	Increased **accountability for student performance**, emphasizing data-driven instruction.
2004	Reauthorization of IDEA	Introduced **Response to Intervention (RTI)** as a method for identifying learning disabilities.
2015	Every Student Succeeds Act (ESSA)	Encouraged **multi-tiered approaches** to support both academic and behavioral interventions.

MTSS emerged as a comprehensive framework that integrates RTI, PBIS, and other evidence-based practices to create a unified system of support for all students.

Understanding the Core Components of MTSS

At its core, MTSS is a proactive and systematic approach to identifying and addressing students' academic, behavioral, and social-emotional needs. The framework consists of several essential components:

1. Tiered System of Support

MTSS organizes instruction and intervention into three tiers, with increasing levels of intensity based on student needs.

Figure 2.2: The Three-Tiered Model of MTSS

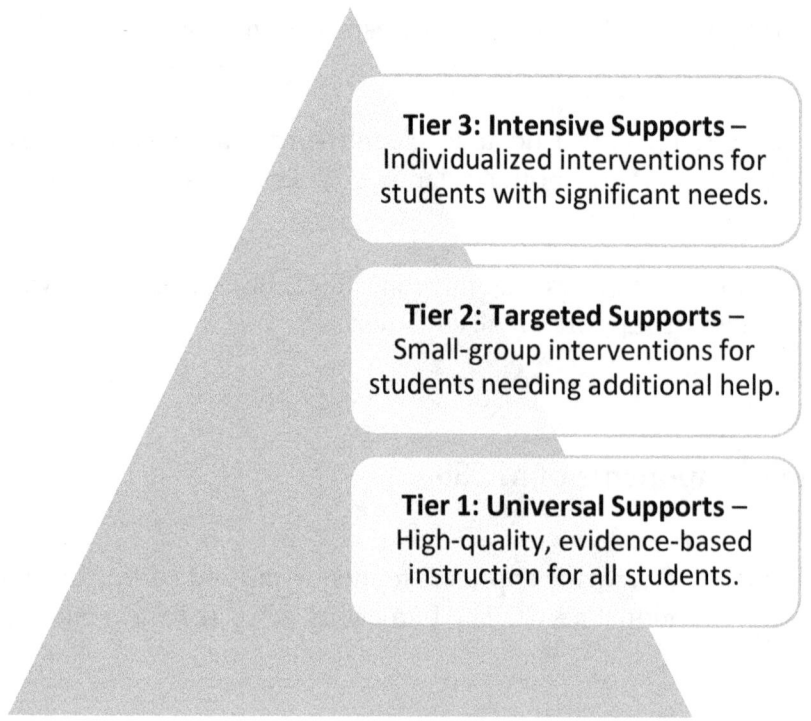

This tiered approach ensures that every student receives the right level of support at the right time.

2. Data-Driven Decision-Making

MTSS relies on **continuous data collection and analysis** to guide intervention decisions. Educators use:

- ✓ **Universal Screening Assessments** to identify students at risk.
- ✓ **Progress Monitoring Tools** to track student growth over time.
- ✓ **Diagnostic Assessments** to pinpoint specific skill deficits.

By using data to inform instruction, educators can ensure that interventions are targeted and effective.

3. Collaborative Problem-Solving Teams

MTSS is not implemented in isolation—it requires collaboration among educators, specialists, and administrators. Schools establish MTSS problem-solving teams that:

- ✓ Review student data and identify intervention needs.
- ✓ Develop and adjust support plans.
- ✓ Monitor student progress and determine next steps.

Effective teamwork is essential for ensuring consistency in MTSS implementation across grade levels and school sites.

---

4. A Whole-Child Approach: Academic, Behavioral, and Social-Emotional Supports

MTSS extends beyond academics to support behavior and social-emotional well-being. A comprehensive MTSS framework integrates:

- **Academic Interventions** – Differentiated instruction and research-based interventions.
- **Behavioral Interventions (PBIS)** – Positive reinforcement strategies and behavioral supports.
- **Social-Emotional Learning (SEL)** – Counseling, restorative practices, and mental health supports.

This holistic approach ensures that students receive well-rounded support for their overall success.

Distinguishing MTSS from RTI and PBIS

Many educators confuse MTSS with Response to Intervention (RTI) and Positive Behavioral Interventions and Supports (PBIS). While these models share similarities, MTSS is a broader, more comprehensive framework.

Table 2.2: Comparing MTSS, RTI, and PBIS

Framework	Focus Area	Key Characteristics
MTSS	Academic, behavioral, and SEL supports	A **comprehensive, integrated** system for all students.
RTI	Academic interventions	Focuses primarily on **academic skill development** and early intervention.
PBIS	Behavioral supports	Focuses on **preventing and addressing behavioral challenges** through positive reinforcement.

MTSS incorporates RTI and PBIS but extends beyond them to address all aspects of student development.

The Role of Equity in MTSS

A critical goal of MTSS is to ensure that all students have equitable access to high-quality education. Schools must be intentional about culturally responsive instruction, reducing bias in intervention practices, and addressing systemic barriers that impact student success.

Key strategies for promoting equity in MTSS include:

- ✓ **Using data to identify disparities** and ensuring interventions meet diverse student needs.
- ✓ **Providing professional development** on culturally responsive practices.
- ✓ **Engaging families and communities** to support students beyond the school setting.

Equity is not an add-on to MTSS—it is an essential part of building a successful support system for all students.

Conclusion

MTSS serves as the foundation for providing personalized, data-driven support to students in academic, behavioral, and social-emotional domains. By understanding the history, core components, and distinctions between MTSS, RTI, and PBIS, practitioners can implement MTSS with clarity and confidence.

Key takeaways from this section include:

- ✓ MTSS is **a proactive, multi-tiered framework** that integrates academic, behavioral, and social-emotional supports.
- ✓ The **three-tiered system** ensures that all students receive **appropriate levels of intervention** based on their needs.
- ✓ **Data-driven decision-making** is essential for identifying students at risk and adjusting interventions accordingly.
- ✓ **Collaboration among educators, interventionists, and administrators** is critical for MTSS success.
- ✓ **Equity must be a core component** of MTSS to ensure that all students receive the support they need.

The next section will dive deeper into Tiered Instruction and Intervention Strategies, exploring how educators can effectively implement supports at each level of MTSS to maximize student success.

Section 3: Tiered Instruction and Intervention Strategies

Introduction

A core component of Multi-Tiered System of Supports (MTSS) is its tiered instructional framework, which ensures that students receive the right level of support based on their academic, behavioral, and social-emotional needs. This system is designed to be responsive, data-driven, and adaptable to individual student progress.

This section explores the three tiers of MTSS support, detailing best practices for implementing evidence-based instruction and intervention strategies at each level. It also discusses how educators can use data to move students between tiers, ensuring they receive appropriate and timely interventions to promote success.

Key Learning Objectives

By the end of this training module, educators will be able to:

- **Understand the purpose and structure of MTSS's three-tiered framework.**
- **Differentiate between Tier 1, Tier 2, and Tier 3 supports,** including instructional practices at each level.
- **Implement evidence-based interventions** aligned with student needs.
- **Use progress-monitoring data to make informed decisions** about student movement between tiers.
- **Integrate academic, behavioral, and social-emotional strategies** within each tier to provide a holistic approach to student success.

Overview of the Three-Tiered Framework

MTSS operates on a continuum of support, with Tier 1 serving all students, Tier 2 targeting students who need additional help, and Tier 3 providing individualized interventions for those with significant needs.

Figure 2.3: The Three-Tiered Model of MTSS

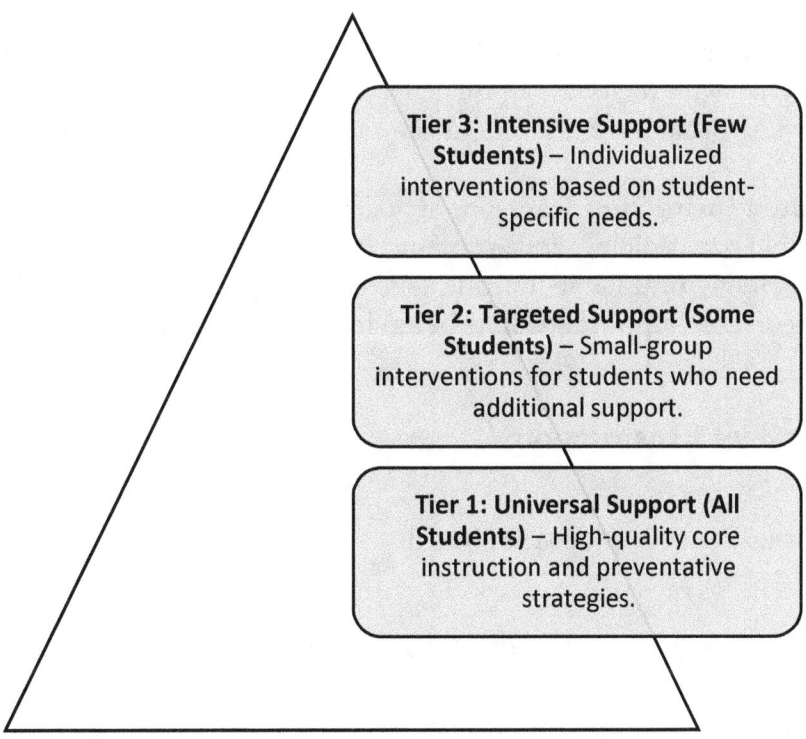

The goal of this model is to provide interventions at increasing levels of intensity, ensuring that all students receive the necessary support before academic failure or behavioral challenges escalate.

Tier 1: Universal Support (Core Instruction for All Students)

Tier 1 represents the foundation of MTSS, consisting of high-quality, evidence-based instruction and proactive supports provided to all students in a general education setting.

Key Characteristics of Tier 1

- ✓ **High-Quality Core Instruction** – All students receive **standards-based, evidence-based teaching** aligned with their developmental and academic needs.
- ✓ **Preventative Approach** – Early identification and intervention **prevent learning gaps before they widen**.
- ✓ **Differentiated Instruction** – Lessons are adapted **to meet diverse learning needs** through flexible grouping, scaffolding, and accommodations.
- ✓ **Schoolwide Behavioral Expectations** – Positive reinforcement strategies, clear expectations, and SEL integration **support student behavior and engagement**.

Best Practices for Tier 1 Instruction

To strengthen Tier 1 instruction, educators should:

- ✓ Use **Universal Design for Learning (UDL)** principles to create **accessible, inclusive lessons**.
- ✓ Implement **active learning strategies**, such as cooperative learning, hands-on activities, and real-world problem-solving.
- ✓ Incorporate **formative assessments** to monitor student progress **in real time**.
- ✓ Provide **embedded social-emotional learning (SEL)** to support students' emotional well-being.

Data Collection at Tier 1

- **Universal Screeners**: Administered **3 times per year** to identify students needing additional support.
- **Classroom Assessments**: Used to gauge progress and adjust instruction as needed.
- **Behavioral Observations**: Monitor student engagement and social-emotional needs.

> **Action Step:** If 80% or more of students are meeting benchmarks at Tier 1, instruction is effective. If fewer than 80% of students are on track, Tier 1 instruction needs improvement before implementing Tier 2 interventions.

Tier 2: Targeted Support (Some Students)

Tier 2 provides additional, small-group instruction for students who do not respond effectively to Tier 1 instruction. These students may not have disabilities but require targeted interventions to close achievement gaps or address behavioral concerns.

Key Characteristics of Tier 2

- ✓ **Small-Group Interventions** – Typically **3-5 students per group**, focused on **specific skill deficits**.
- ✓ **Evidence-Based Interventions** – Explicit, research-backed strategies designed **to accelerate learning**.
- ✓ **Increased Monitoring** – **More frequent progress monitoring** (every 2-4 weeks) to assess intervention effectiveness.
- ✓ **Behavioral and Social-Emotional Supports** – Check-in/check-out systems, mentoring, and self-regulation strategies.

Best Practices for Tier 2 Instruction

- ✓ **Implement explicit, systematic interventions** focused on key skills.
- ✓ **Use diagnostic assessments** to tailor instruction to student needs.
- ✓ **Maintain flexible groupings** based on progress monitoring data.
- ✓ **Ensure interventions are delivered consistently** (e.g., 3-5 sessions per week).

Data Collection at Tier 2

- **Progress Monitoring Assessments**: Administered **every 2-4 weeks** to track student improvement.
- **Intervention Logs**: Document frequency, duration, and response to interventions.
- **Teacher and Student Feedback**: Regular reflection on intervention effectiveness.

> **Action Step:** If a student does not show progress after 6-8 weeks of Tier 2 interventions, consider moving them to Tier 3 for more intensive support.

Tier 3: Intensive Support (Few Students)

Tier 3 provides individualized, intensive interventions for students who have not responded to Tier 1 or Tier 2 supports. These students often require specialized, data-driven interventions to address significant learning or behavioral challenges.

Key Characteristics of Tier 3

- ✓ **One-on-One or Very Small-Group Interventions** – Highly individualized instruction based on diagnostic assessments.
- ✓ **Intensive and Frequent Support** – Sessions occur **4-5 times per week** for **30-60 minutes**.
- ✓ **Specialized, Multi-Disciplinary Teams** – Collaboration between **teachers, interventionists, psychologists, and specialists**.
- ✓ **Behavioral and Mental Health Interventions** – Counseling, therapeutic support, and **Functional Behavior Assessments (FBA)** as needed.

Best Practices for Tier 3 Instruction

- ✓ **Develop individualized intervention plans** based on **root-cause analysis**.
- ✓ Use **explicit instruction, direct modeling, and scaffolding**.
- ✓ **Integrate family involvement** to reinforce strategies at home.
- ✓ **Modify intensity and duration** as needed based on student progress.

Data Collection at Tier 3

- Weekly or bi-weekly **progress monitoring** to assess intervention effectiveness.
- **Individualized data reviews** to determine next steps.
- **Collaboration with specialists** to refine strategies.

> **Action Step:** If Tier 3 interventions do not result in significant progress, the student may be referred for additional evaluations, such as special education services or alternative support plans.

Conclusion

Effective MTSS implementation requires a clear understanding of tiered instruction and intervention strategies.

- ✓ **Tier 1 focuses on high-quality, differentiated instruction** for all students.
- ✓ **Tier 2 provides targeted small-group interventions** for students at risk.
- ✓ **Tier 3 delivers intensive, individualized support** for students with the greatest needs.

By using evidence-based interventions, frequent data collection, and collaborative decision-making, schools can ensure that all students receive the right level of support to succeed.

The next section will explore Data-Driven Decision-Making in MTSS, detailing how educators can use screening, progress monitoring, and diagnostic data to refine interventions and ensure student success.

Section 4: Data-Driven Decision-Making in MTSS

Introduction

A key component of a successful Multi-Tiered System of Supports (MTSS) framework is the use of data to drive instructional and intervention decisions. Educators need to systematically collect, analyze, and apply student data to ensure that interventions are timely, effective, and responsive to individual needs. Without a data-driven approach, interventions may be misaligned, inconsistent, or ineffective, leading to missed opportunities for student growth.

This section explores the role of universal screening, progress monitoring, and diagnostic assessments in MTSS decision-making. It also highlights best practices for data interpretation, collaboration, and response to student progress, ensuring that educators can use data to make informed instructional adjustments.

Key Learning Objectives

By the end of this training module, educators will be able to:

- **Understand the role of data in MTSS** and why it is essential for student success.
- **Differentiate between universal screening, progress monitoring, and diagnostic assessments.**
- **Use data to identify student needs** and determine appropriate interventions.
- **Interpret assessment results effectively** to guide decision-making.
- **Collaborate with colleagues** to analyze student progress and refine instructional strategies.

The Role of Data in MTSS

MTSS is fundamentally a data-driven framework, requiring continuous assessment and refinement of instructional practices. The data collection process serves three primary functions:

1. **Identifying students who need additional support** (universal screening).
2. **Monitoring student progress over time** (progress monitoring).
3. **Diagnosing specific learning or behavioral needs** (diagnostic assessments).

To ensure that MTSS interventions are proactive rather than reactive, educators must follow a structured, ongoing data cycle that informs decision-making at every tier.

Figure 2.4: The MTSS Data Cycle

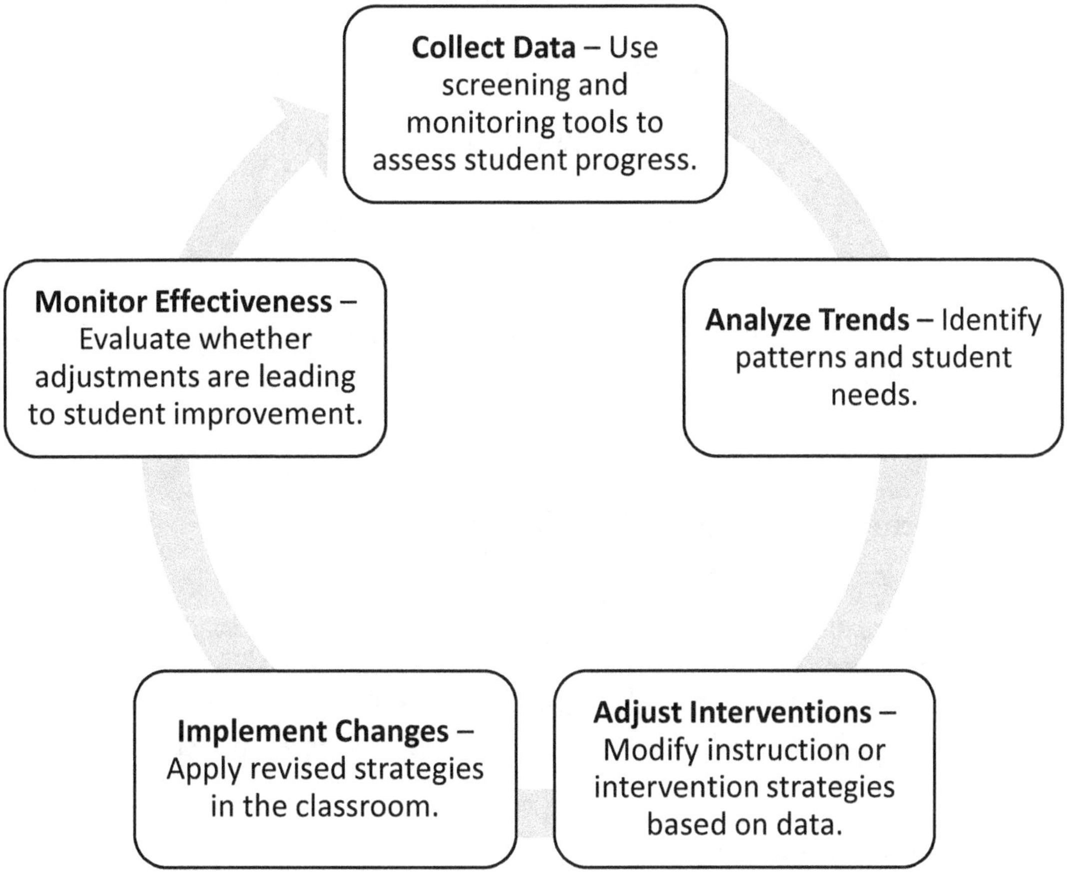

Collect Data – Use screening and monitoring tools to assess student progress.

Analyze Trends – Identify patterns and student needs.

Adjust Interventions – Modify instruction or intervention strategies based on data.

Implement Changes – Apply revised strategies in the classroom.

Monitor Effectiveness – Evaluate whether adjustments are leading to student improvement.

This continuous cycle ensures that MTSS interventions remain dynamic and responsive, rather than static and predetermined.

Key Types of Data Collection in MTSS

Data in MTSS falls into three primary categories, each serving a distinct purpose in student support:

1. Universal Screening: Identifying At-Risk Students

- ✓ **What It Is:** A school-wide assessment given to all students to identify those who may be struggling academically, behaviorally, or socially.
- ✓ **When It Happens:** Typically three times per year (fall, winter, spring).
- ✓ **Why It Matters:** Ensures that no student slips through the cracks by identifying concerns before they become major challenges.

Common Universal Screeners

Area	Common Assessments Used
Reading	DIBELS, STAR Reading, AIMSweb
Math	iReady, NWEA MAP, EasyCBM
Behavior/Social-Emotional	BASC-3 BESS, SRSS-IE, SAEBRS

➤ **Action Step:** If a student scores below the benchmark, they are flagged for Tier 2 or Tier 3 interventions, depending on the severity of need.

---

2. Progress Monitoring: Tracking Student Growth

- ✓ **What It Is:** A method of frequent, targeted assessment used to track how well students are responding to interventions.
- ✓ **When It Happens:** Every 2-4 weeks (Tier 2) or weekly (Tier 3).
- ✓ **Why It Matters:** Helps educators adjust interventions in real time to ensure effectiveness.

Best Practices for Progress Monitoring

- ✓ Use **brief, skill-specific assessments** rather than lengthy tests.
- ✓ Ensure monitoring is **consistent and scheduled**, rather than sporadic.
- ✓ Analyze **rate of improvement (ROI)** to determine intervention success.
- ➤ **Action Step:** If a student is not making adequate progress after 6-8 weeks of intervention, the team should modify the intervention or consider Tier 3 support.

---

3. Diagnostic Assessments: Pinpointing Root Causes

- ✓ **What It Is:** In-depth assessments used to identify specific skill deficits, learning disabilities, or behavioral concerns.
- ✓ **When It Happens:** After a student is flagged as not responding to Tier 2 or Tier 3 interventions.
- ✓ **Why It Matters:** Helps tailor interventions to student-specific needs rather than using a one-size-fits-all approach.

Examples of Diagnostic Assessments

Assessment Type	Common Examples
Reading Diagnostics	Phonological Awareness Screening Test (PAST), QRI-5
Math Diagnostics	KeyMath-3, Woodcock-Johnson Tests of Achievement
Behavioral Diagnostics	Functional Behavior Assessment (FBA), Social Skills Improvement System (SSIS)

> **Action Step:** Diagnostic data should be used to inform Individualized Education Programs (IEPs) if special education services are considered.

Using Data to Drive Instructional Decisions

Once data is collected, it must be used effectively to inform instructional changes. The following strategies help educators make data-informed decisions that improve student outcomes.

1. Data-Based Decision-Making Meetings

Regular MTSS team meetings should be held to:

- ✓ Review student data **every 6-8 weeks.**
- ✓ **Identify students who need additional support.**
- ✓ Adjust intervention plans based on progress monitoring results.
- ✓ Ensure interventions align with student-specific needs.
- ❖ **Example in Practice:** A school schedules bi-weekly MTSS data meetings, where teachers and interventionists review student progress and make collaborative decisions on next steps.

2. Differentiated Intervention Adjustments

If data shows that an intervention is not working, adjustments should be made. The following table outlines how to modify interventions based on progress data.

Table 2.3: Adjusting Interventions Based on Progress Monitoring Data

Progress Trend	Instructional Decision
Rapid improvement	Consider reducing intervention frequency or moving student back to Tier 1.
Steady progress	Continue intervention as planned.
Minimal progress	Modify intervention strategy (e.g., increase duration, change instructional method).
No progress	Conduct diagnostic assessment and consider Tier 3 or special education referral.

3. Visualizing Data to Guide Conversations

Educators can use data dashboards, color-coded spreadsheets, or student progress graphs to quickly interpret student growth patterns.

> ➤ **Action Step:** Schools should train teachers on how to interpret data visually to make decision-making more efficient and transparent.

Conclusion

Data-driven decision-making is the backbone of effective MTSS implementation. By using universal screening, progress monitoring, and diagnostic assessments, educators can ensure that students receive the right support at the right time.

Key takeaways from this section include:

- ✓ **Universal screening** identifies students who need interventions.
- ✓ **Progress monitoring** tracks student response to interventions over time.
- ✓ **Diagnostic assessments** help refine and personalize interventions.
- ✓ **Regular MTSS data meetings** ensure interventions remain targeted and effective.
- ✓ **Data visualization tools** help educators make sense of complex student progress trends.

The next section will explore Collaboration and Team-Based Problem-Solving in MTSS, highlighting how educators, specialists, and administrators can work together to make informed, student-centered decisions.

Section 5: Collaboration and Team-Based Problem-Solving in MTSS

Introduction

MTSS is not a framework that operates in isolation—it thrives on collaborative, team-based problem-solving. Effective implementation requires a coordinated effort among general educators, interventionists, administrators, special education staff, counselors, and families. When collaboration is structured, data-driven, and goal-oriented, it ensures that students receive the right support at the right time.

This section explores best practices for establishing and maintaining effective MTSS teams, structuring problem-solving meetings, and fostering a culture of shared responsibility in student success.

Key Learning Objectives

By the end of this training module, educators will be able to:

- **Understand the role of collaboration in MTSS** and why teamwork is essential.
- **Define the key roles and responsibilities of MTSS team members.**
- **Establish structured problem-solving protocols** to guide MTSS discussions.
- **Engage in effective data-driven decision-making** as a collaborative team.
- **Communicate with families and external stakeholders** to ensure wraparound student support.

The Role of Collaboration in MTSS

MTSS functions as a multi-disciplinary system that integrates academic, behavioral, and social-emotional interventions. Each team member plays a unique role, and collaboration ensures that students benefit from diverse expertise and perspectives.

Without effective teamwork, MTSS can become disjointed, inconsistent, and inefficient, leading to poor intervention implementation and misaligned student support plans.

Benefits of Collaboration in MTSS

- ✓ **More comprehensive student support** – Interdisciplinary teams address students' academic, behavioral, and social-emotional needs holistically.
- ✓ **Increased consistency across grade levels** – Ensures that interventions and supports are aligned school-wide.
- ✓ **More informed decision-making** – Team discussions lead to better intervention choices based on multiple perspectives.
- ✓ **Improved intervention fidelity** – Shared responsibility increases accountability and follow-through on MTSS plans.

Challenges in MTSS Collaboration

Despite the benefits, MTSS teamwork can face obstacles such as:

- ✖ **Lack of clear roles** – Educators may be unsure of their responsibilities within the team.
- ✖ **Ineffective communication** – Miscommunication can lead to inconsistent implementation.
- ✖ **Limited meeting time** – Schools may struggle to find time for structured, meaningful collaboration.
- ✖ **Resistance to shared decision-making** – Some educators may be hesitant to embrace a team-based approach.

Addressing these challenges requires well-defined team roles, structured meeting protocols, and a culture of collaboration.

Key MTSS Team Roles and Responsibilities

Each member of an MTSS team brings a unique skill set and perspective to the table. The following table outlines common roles and their primary contributions to MTSS implementation.

Table 2.4: MTSS Team Roles and Responsibilities

Team Member	Key Responsibilities in MTSS
General Educators	Implement Tier 1 instruction, identify struggling students, collect classroom data, and collaborate on interventions.
Interventionists	Provide targeted Tier 2 & Tier 3 support, track student progress, and recommend evidence-based strategies.
Special Educators	Assist in identifying students with disabilities, ensure compliance with IEPs, and provide specialized instruction.
Administrators	Oversee MTSS implementation, allocate resources, and support professional development.
School Psychologists	Conduct diagnostic assessments, provide behavioral support strategies, and consult on student mental health.
Counselors & Social Workers	Address social-emotional needs, facilitate student support groups, and communicate with families.
Parents & Guardians	Partner with the school team to support student progress at home and advocate for their child's needs.

➢ **Action Step:** Schools should clearly define these roles in their MTSS handbook or implementation plan to ensure alignment and clarity.

Structuring Effective MTSS Team Meetings

To maximize efficiency and impact, MTSS meetings should be structured, goal-oriented, and data-driven. Without clear protocols, meetings can become unfocused, reactive, and ineffective.

Best Practices for MTSS Team Meetings

- ✓ **Use a Set Agenda** – Meetings should follow a consistent structure to stay focused.
- ✓ **Make Data the Centerpiece** – All discussions should be grounded in student data.
- ✓ **Document Action Items** – Clearly assign next steps and responsibilities to each team member.
- ✓ **Ensure Equal Participation** – Encourage all voices to be heard, including general educators, specialists, and parents.
- ✓ **Schedule Meetings in Advance** – Regular, pre-planned meetings prevent scheduling conflicts and last-minute cancellations.

The MTSS Problem-Solving Process

When a student is struggling, the MTSS team must engage in structured problem-solving to determine the appropriate interventions. This involves a four-step process to analyze student needs and develop an effective support plan.

Figure 2.5: The MTSS Problem-Solving Cycle

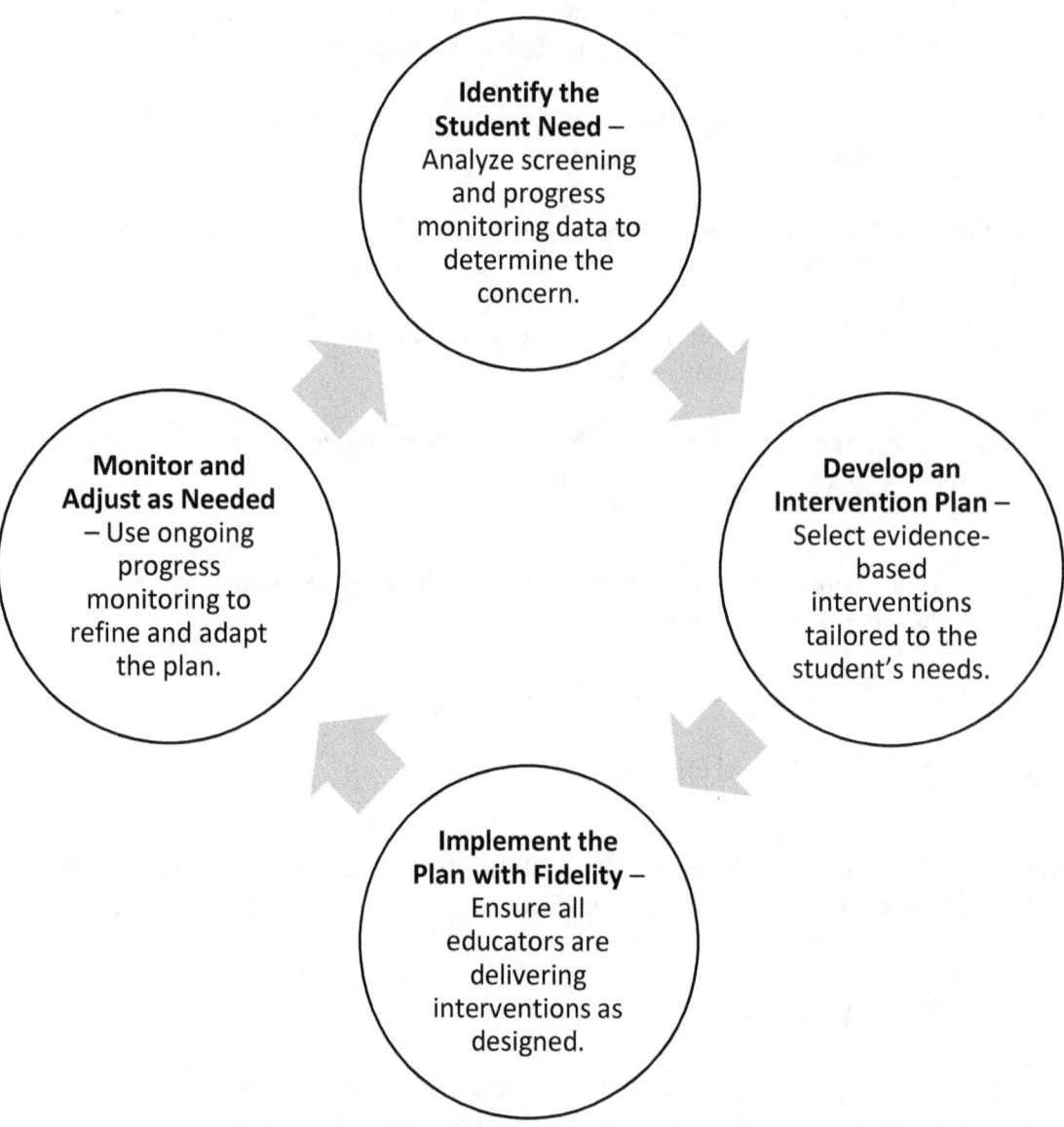

This structured approach prevents guesswork and subjective decision-making, ensuring that student support is systematic and data-driven.

Fostering Family and Community Partnerships in MTSS

MTSS is most effective when schools engage families as active partners in the intervention process. Parents and guardians can provide valuable insights into a student's needs, strengths, and challenges that educators may not observe in school.

Best Practices for Family Collaboration

- ✓ **Communicate Early and Often** – Keep families informed before problems escalate.
- ✓ **Use Clear, Jargon-Free Language** – Explain MTSS interventions in plain terms so parents understand the process.
- ✓ **Offer Multiple Communication Channels** – Use email, phone calls, parent meetings, and digital platforms to maintain consistent engagement.
- ✓ **Provide Home-Based Strategies** – Share practical ways families can reinforce interventions at home.
- ✓ **Respect Cultural and Linguistic Diversity** – Ensure communication is inclusive and accessible to all families.
- ➢ **Action Step:** Schools should create a family MTSS guide that explains the framework and how parents can get involved in the support process.

Conclusion

Collaboration is at the heart of successful MTSS implementation. Without effective teamwork, intervention efforts can become fragmented and inconsistent, leading to inequitable student support.

Key takeaways from this section include:

- ✓ **Clearly defined team roles** ensure accountability and alignment.
- ✓ **Structured, data-driven meetings** improve intervention effectiveness.
- ✓ **The MTSS problem-solving cycle** provides a clear process for decision-making.
- ✓ **Family engagement is essential** to support student growth beyond the school setting.

By fostering a culture of shared responsibility and collaboration, schools can create a cohesive, student-centered MTSS system that maximizes outcomes for all learners.

The next section will explore Culturally Responsive and Equity-Based MTSS Practices, focusing on strategies to ensure that MTSS interventions meet the needs of diverse learners and promote educational equity.

Section 6: Culturally Responsive and Equity-Based MTSS Practices

Introduction

Ensuring that MTSS serves all students equitably is essential for its success. Historically, educational systems have struggled to provide consistent, high-quality support for diverse learners, often resulting in disparities in academic achievement, discipline, and access to resources. A culturally responsive and equity-based MTSS framework ensures that interventions and supports are designed to meet the unique needs of students from all racial, ethnic, linguistic, and socioeconomic backgrounds.

This section explores the importance of equity in MTSS, best practices for culturally responsive teaching, and strategies for reducing bias in data collection, intervention practices, and disciplinary actions.

Key Learning Objectives

By the end of this training module, educators will be able to:

- **Understand the role of equity in MTSS** and why culturally responsive practices are critical.
- **Identify systemic barriers** that contribute to disparities in student outcomes.
- **Implement culturally responsive instructional and intervention strategies.**
- **Reduce bias in MTSS data collection and decision-making.**
- **Promote an inclusive school climate** that values student identity and diversity.

The Role of Equity in MTSS

MTSS is designed to provide personalized support to students based on their needs. However, without an intentional focus on equity, the system can unintentionally reinforce disparities rather than close achievement gaps.

Why Equity Matters in MTSS

- ✓ **Prevents overidentification in special education** – Historically, students of color—particularly Black and Latino males—have been disproportionately placed in special education due to biased intervention practices and assessments.
- ✓ **Reduces exclusionary discipline practices** – Students from marginalized backgrounds **receive suspensions and expulsions at higher rates**, limiting their access to learning.
- ✓ **Ensures access to high-quality interventions** – All students should receive culturally responsive instruction and interventions that reflect their lived experiences.
- ✓ **Builds stronger relationships between educators and students** – Culturally responsive teaching fosters trust, belonging, and engagement in learning.
- ➤ **Action Step:** Schools should conduct equity audits to assess how student demographics correlate with intervention placements, discipline rates, and academic outcomes.

Identifying Systemic Barriers in MTSS

Before schools can implement culturally responsive MTSS practices, they must first recognize the **barriers that contribute to inequitable student experiences**.

Common Barriers to Equity in MTSS

Barrier	Impact on Students
Implicit Bias in Referrals	Educators may **misinterpret cultural differences** as academic or behavioral deficits.
One-Size-Fits-All Interventions	Standardized interventions may not address **linguistic and cultural differences** in learning styles.
Limited Representation in Curriculum	Lack of diverse texts and learning materials **reduces student engagement and relevance**.
Disproportionate Discipline Practices	Subjective behavioral expectations can **lead to higher discipline rates for marginalized students**.
Lack of Multilingual Support	English learners (ELs) may not receive **adequate intervention in their home language**.

- ➤ **Action Step:** Schools should review MTSS data **disaggregated by race, language, and socioeconomic status** to identify disparities in intervention access and student outcomes.

Implementing Culturally Responsive Teaching and Intervention Strategies

Culturally responsive teaching (CRT) is an essential component of an equitable MTSS framework. It ensures that instruction, interventions, and behavioral supports are designed with students' cultural backgrounds, lived experiences, and linguistic needs in mind.

Key Principles of Culturally Responsive Teaching in MTSS

- ✓ **Asset-Based Mindset** – Recognizing that all students bring valuable knowledge and experiences to the learning process.
- ✓ **Linguistic Inclusion** – Supporting students in both their native language and English when delivering interventions.
- ✓ **Representation in Curriculum** – Incorporating diverse perspectives and cultural narratives in instructional materials.
- ✓ **Flexible Teaching Approaches** – Differentiating instruction based on students' learning styles and cultural contexts.
- ✓ **Family and Community Engagement** – Partnering with families to incorporate culturally relevant strategies into intervention plans.

Examples of Culturally Responsive Strategies in MTSS

MTSS Area	Culturally Responsive Strategy
Tier 1 (Universal Instruction)	Use **culturally relevant texts**, incorporate students' backgrounds into lessons.
Tier 2 (Targeted Intervention)	Offer **language support** for English learners, provide intervention examples that reflect students' lived experiences.
Tier 3 (Intensive Support)	Conduct **linguistically appropriate diagnostic assessments**, engage family members in goal-setting.

- ➢ **Action Step:** Schools should provide ongoing professional development on culturally responsive practices to ensure all educators are trained in equity-based MTSS strategies.

Reducing Bias in MTSS Data Collection and Decision-Making

Unconscious bias can influence how educators interpret data, identify struggling students, and recommend interventions. Without safeguards, data-driven decisions in MTSS can reinforce inequities rather than resolve them.

Best Practices for Reducing Bias in MTSS Data

- ✓ **Use Multiple Data Sources** – Rely on a combination of quantitative (test scores) and qualitative (observations, student voice) data to make decisions.
- ✓ **Establish Clear Referral Criteria** – Ensure that all students are evaluated based on the same objective criteria rather than subjective perceptions.
- ✓ **Train Educators on Implicit Bias** – Provide PD on how bias affects student identification for interventions.
- ✓ **Review Data for Disproportionality** – Compare MTSS data across racial, linguistic, and socioeconomic groups to detect patterns of inequity.
- ✓ **Engage Families in the Data Process** – Give parents access to their child's data and a role in intervention decision-making.
- ➤ **Action Step:** Schools should create equity-focused MTSS data review teams that analyze intervention patterns and ensure that all students receive fair, appropriate support.

Promoting an Inclusive and Culturally Affirming School Climate

Beyond instruction and interventions, schools must create an environment where all students feel safe, valued, and included.

Strategies for Building an Inclusive MTSS Culture

- ✓ **Culturally Responsive PBIS (Positive Behavioral Interventions and Supports)** – Ensure that behavioral expectations reflect student backgrounds and community values.
- ✓ **Restorative Practices Instead of Punitive Discipline** – Use conflict resolution strategies, peer mediation, and student-led discussions instead of suspensions.
- ✓ **Student Voice in Decision-Making** – Involve students in shaping MTSS policies, behavioral expectations, and school culture initiatives.
- ✓ **Cultural Competency Training for Staff** – Provide PD focused on anti-racism, trauma-informed practices, and cultural humility.
- ➤ **Action Step:** Schools should conduct **student and family surveys to assess school climate and cultural inclusivity within MTSS implementation.**

Conclusion

Equity must be a central pillar of MTSS, ensuring that all students—regardless of race, language, or background—receive the support they need to succeed.

Key takeaways from this section include:

- ✓ **Equity in MTSS prevents systemic barriers** from affecting student outcomes.
- ✓ **Culturally responsive teaching** enhances intervention effectiveness.
- ✓ **Bias in data collection and referrals must be addressed** to ensure fair decision-making.
- ✓ **Building an inclusive school climate** strengthens MTSS implementation.

By integrating culturally responsive and equity-based practices, schools create a more just, effective, and student-centered MTSS system.

The next section will explore Behavioral and Social-Emotional Supports in MTSS, detailing strategies for integrating PBIS, mental health services, and trauma-informed practices into a comprehensive support framework.

Section 7: Behavioral and Social-Emotional Supports in MTSS

Introduction

Multi-Tiered System of Supports (MTSS) extends beyond academics to include behavioral and social-emotional supports that address the whole child. Many students struggle not only with academic content but also with behavioral expectations, self-regulation, emotional well-being, and mental health challenges. Without proper behavioral and social-emotional support, students may struggle to engage in learning and develop positive relationships.

Integrating Positive Behavioral Interventions and Supports (PBIS), Social-Emotional Learning (SEL), and mental health resources within MTSS ensures that students receive preventative, targeted, and intensive support for both behavior and emotional development. This section explores how schools can embed behavioral and SEL strategies into MTSS tiers, ensuring all students have access to a safe, supportive, and inclusive learning environment.

Key Learning Objectives

By the end of this training module, educators will be able to:

- Understand the importance of behavioral and social-emotional supports in MTSS.
- **Differentiate between PBIS, SEL, and mental health interventions** within the MTSS framework.
- **Implement tiered behavioral and SEL supports** that align with student needs.
- Use data to monitor student behavior and emotional well-being.
- **Engage in trauma-informed and restorative practices** to create a positive school climate.

Integrating PBIS, SEL, and Mental Health Support in MTSS

MTSS behavioral and social-emotional supports are not separate systems—they are integrated within the tiered framework alongside academic interventions. Schools that successfully implement MTSS focus on proactive strategies, early intervention, and targeted mental health supports.

Key Components of Behavioral and SEL Supports in MTSS

- ✓ **PBIS (Positive Behavioral Interventions and Supports)** – A proactive framework that teaches and reinforces expected behaviors while minimizing punitive discipline.
- ✓ **Social-Emotional Learning (SEL)** – Instruction that helps students develop self-awareness, emotional regulation, social skills, and responsible decision-making.
- ✓ **Trauma-Informed Practices** – Ensuring that student interventions consider past experiences and provide emotional safety.
- ✓ **Mental Health Supports** – School-based counseling, mental health screenings, and intervention programs to address students' well-being.
- ➢ **Action Step:** Schools should establish **a unified approach that integrates PBIS, SEL, and mental health services within the MTSS framework.**

Tiered Behavioral and Social-Emotional Supports

Just as academic instruction follows a tiered model, behavioral and social-emotional supports should be structured to match student needs.

Figure 2.6: Tiered Behavioral and SEL Supports in MTSS

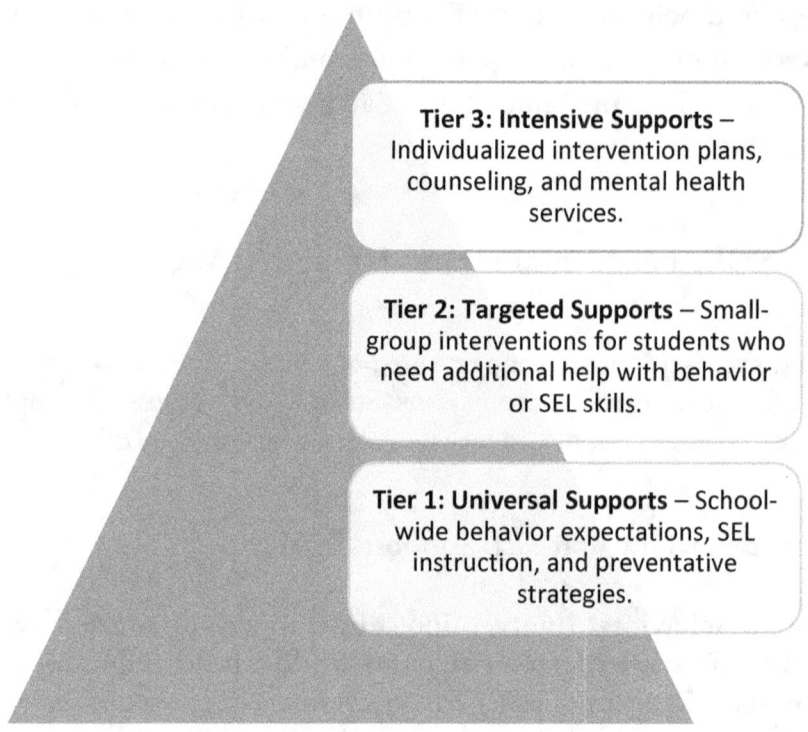

Each tier ensures that students receive appropriate levels of support based on their behavioral and social-emotional needs.

Tier 1: Universal Behavioral and SEL Supports (All Students)

Tier 1 serves as the foundation for all students by promoting positive behavior, social-emotional learning, and school-wide expectations.

Key Components of Tier 1 Behavioral Supports

- ✓ **PBIS Schoolwide Expectations** – Clearly define and teach positive behavioral expectations (e.g., Be Respectful, Be Responsible, Be Safe).
- ✓ **Explicit SEL Instruction** – Incorporate SEL lessons into the curriculum using research-based programs (e.g., CASEL's five SEL competencies).
- ✓ **Restorative Practices** – Shift from punitive discipline to relationship-building and conflict resolution.
- ✓ **Classroom Management Strategies** – Implement consistent routines, positive reinforcement, and de-escalation techniques.

Best Practices for Tier 1 Implementation

- ✓ **Teach behavioral expectations at the start of the year and reinforce them consistently.**
- ✓ **Use classroom circles and SEL check-ins to support students' emotional regulation.**
- ✓ **Monitor school-wide behavioral data to identify trends and adjust supports as needed.**
- ➢ **Action Step:** If 80% of students follow behavioral expectations, Tier 1 is effective. If not, Tier 1 supports need to be strengthened before adding Tier 2 interventions.

Tier 2: Targeted Behavioral and SEL Supports (Some Students)

Tier 2 provides additional support for students who struggle with behavior or social-emotional skills despite universal Tier 1 supports.

Key Components of Tier 2 Behavioral Supports

- ✓ **Small-Group SEL Instruction** – Focused lessons on self-regulation, conflict resolution, and coping strategies.
- ✓ **Check-In/Check-Out (CICO)** – Daily goal-setting and mentoring with an assigned adult.
- ✓ **Behavior Contracts & Self-Monitoring** – Personalized strategies to help students track progress.
- ✓ **Short-Term Counseling or Support Groups** – Targeted interventions for students experiencing anxiety, trauma, or peer-related challenges.

Best Practices for Tier 2 Implementation

- ✓ Ensure interventions are implemented consistently (e.g., at least 3x per week).
- ✓ Use progress monitoring tools to assess student response to interventions.
- ✓ Keep parents informed and involve them in reinforcing behavioral goals at home.
- ➢ **Action Step:** If students do not show improvement after 6-8 weeks, adjust interventions or consider Tier 3 supports.

Tier 3: Intensive Behavioral and SEL Supports (Few Students)

Tier 3 interventions are for students with significant behavioral, social-emotional, or mental health needs. These students require individualized support plans that go beyond Tier 1 and Tier 2 strategies.

Key Components of Tier 3 Behavioral Supports

- ✓ **Individualized Behavior Intervention Plans (BIPs)** – Data-driven plans that address specific behaviors with tailored supports.
- ✓ **One-on-One Counseling or Therapy** – Intensive mental health support for students with anxiety, depression, trauma, or emotional dysregulation.
- ✓ **Functional Behavior Assessment (FBA)** – Identifying root causes of behavior and designing interventions accordingly.
- ✓ **Crisis Intervention Plans** – Safety plans for students in distress or at risk of harm.

Best Practices for Tier 3 Implementation

- ✓ Use highly individualized, research-based interventions.
- ✓ Ensure frequent progress monitoring (e.g., weekly data collection).
- ✓ Collaborate with school psychologists, social workers, and external mental health professionals.
- ➢ **Action Step:** If a student does not respond to Tier 3 interventions, a referral for special education services or external mental health support may be necessary.

Using Data to Monitor Behavior and Social-Emotional Growth

Just as academic interventions rely on data, behavioral and SEL supports require continuous monitoring.

Key Data Sources for Behavioral and SEL Progress Monitoring

- ✓ **Office Discipline Referrals (ODRs)** – Tracks school-wide behavior trends.
- ✓ **Behavioral Progress Monitoring Forms** – Teacher and student self-reports on goal progress.
- ✓ **Social-Emotional Screening Tools** – SAEBRS, DESSA, or BASC-3 BESS assessments.
- ✓ **Student and Family Surveys** – Collects qualitative data on school climate and student well-being.
- ➢ **Action Step:** Schools should review behavioral and SEL data monthly to adjust interventions as needed.

Conclusion

Behavioral and social-emotional supports must be embedded within the MTSS framework to ensure that students receive comprehensive, whole-child support.

Key takeaways from this section include:

- ✓ PBIS, SEL, and mental health supports must be integrated into MTSS.
- ✓ Tiered interventions ensure that all students receive appropriate behavioral and SEL support.
- ✓ Progress monitoring and data collection are essential for refining interventions.
- ✓ Restorative practices and trauma-informed approaches create safer, more inclusive school environments.

The next chapter will explore assessing the effectiveness of MTSS professional development, ensuring that training efforts lead to improved educator practice and student success.

Chapter 3: Assessing the Effectiveness of MTSS Professional Development

Section 1: Chapter Overview

Introduction to the Chapter's Focus

The effectiveness of Multi-Tiered System of Supports (MTSS) depends heavily on high-quality professional development (PD) for educators, interventionists, administrators, and support staff. However, providing PD alone is not enough—schools and districts must assess whether professional development efforts lead to meaningful improvements in educator practice and student outcomes.

This chapter explores how to measure the impact of MTSS professional development, using a combination of quantitative and qualitative evaluation methods. It outlines key performance indicators (KPIs), feedback mechanisms, and data-driven assessment strategies to ensure that professional learning leads to sustained implementation and student success.

Key Objectives and Learning Outcomes

By the end of this chapter, readers will be able to:

- **Understand the importance of assessing MTSS professional development effectiveness.**
- **Identify key metrics for measuring the impact of training.**
- **Use multiple assessment methods, including participant feedback, implementation fidelity checks, and student progress data.**
- **Adjust professional development strategies based on data-driven insights.**
- **Develop a continuous improvement model** for MTSS training initiatives.

To provide an overview of the evaluation areas, **Figure 3.1 illustrates the core components** of MTSS professional development assessment.

Figure 3.1: Essential Components of MTSS Professional Development Evaluation

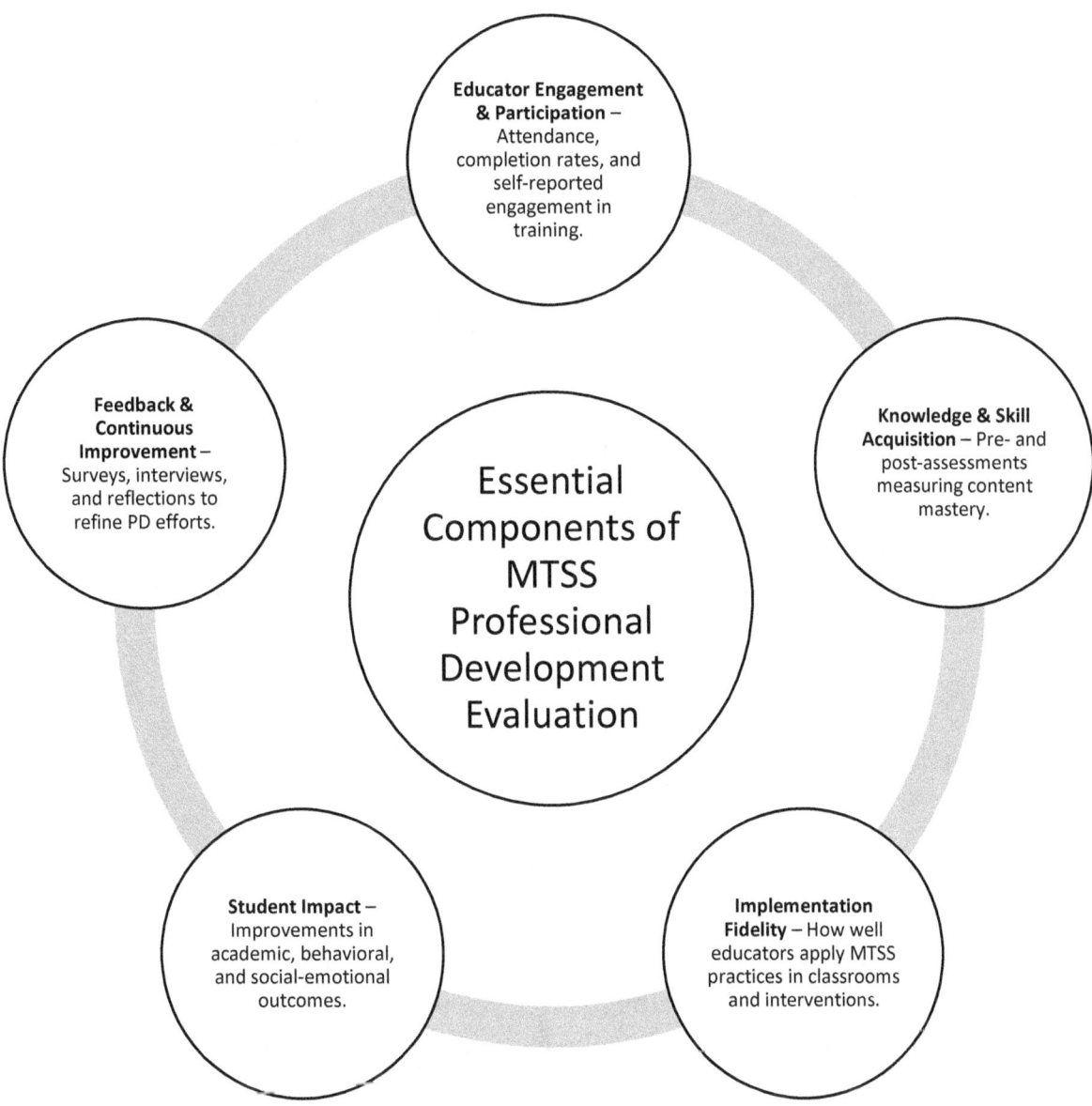

Each of these elements plays a critical role in determining the success of MTSS professional development and ensuring that training translates into real-world application.

In the next section, we will explore theoretical models for professional development evaluation, including frameworks by Guskey (2000) and Kirkpatrick (1994) that provide structured approaches for assessing training effectiveness.

Section 2: Theoretical Models for Evaluating Professional Development

Introduction

Assessing the effectiveness of professional development (PD) in Multi-Tiered System of Supports (MTSS) requires a structured, research-based approach. Simply tracking attendance at training sessions does not provide insight into whether educators are effectively implementing learned strategies or if students are benefiting from improved instruction and interventions.

This section explores two widely recognized models for evaluating professional learning:

1. **Guskey's Five Levels of Professional Development Evaluation (2000)**
2. **Kirkpatrick's Four Levels of Training Evaluation (1994)**

Both frameworks provide a multi-tiered approach to measuring the short-term and long-term impact of professional learning, ensuring that PD efforts lead to sustained changes in educator practice and student outcomes.

Key Learning Objectives

By the end of this training module, educators and administrators will be able to:

- **Understand the importance of structured PD evaluation models.**
- **Apply Guskey's Five Levels of Evaluation** to assess the impact of MTSS training.
- **Use Kirkpatrick's Four Levels of Training Evaluation** to measure engagement, learning, behavior change, and student outcomes.
- **Select appropriate assessment tools** for measuring PD effectiveness.
- **Use evaluation data to refine and improve future MTSS professional learning initiatives.**

Guskey's Five Levels of Professional Development Evaluation (2000)

Thomas Guskey (2000) developed a comprehensive model for evaluating PD effectiveness that extends beyond simple participant satisfaction. This model assesses PD impact at five levels, ranging from immediate reactions to long-term student achievement gains.

Table 3.1: Guskey's Five Levels of Professional Development Evaluation

Level	Focus Area	Evaluation Methods
Level 1: Participant Reactions	How educators feel about the PD experience (engagement, relevance, usefulness).	Post-session surveys, participant feedback forms.
Level 2: Learning Outcomes	What knowledge and skills educators gained from training.	Pre- and post-assessments, knowledge quizzes, reflection journals.
Level 3: Organizational Support & Change	How well the school/district supports implementation (time, resources, coaching).	Leadership interviews, PD implementation surveys, focus groups.
Level 4: Educator Application	How effectively educators apply new knowledge and skills in practice.	Classroom observations, fidelity checklists, peer coaching feedback.
Level 5: Student Impact	How PD improves student learning, behavior, and engagement.	Student progress monitoring data, academic achievement scores, behavioral incident reports.

> ➤ **Action Step:** Schools should use a combination of these evaluation methods to assess both the short-term effectiveness and long-term impact of MTSS PD.

Kirkpatrick's Four Levels of Training Evaluation (1994)

Kirkpatrick's model provides another structured approach to evaluating professional learning by assessing four levels of impact, from immediate reactions to broader organizational change.

Figure 3.2: Kirkpatrick's Four Levels of Training Evaluation

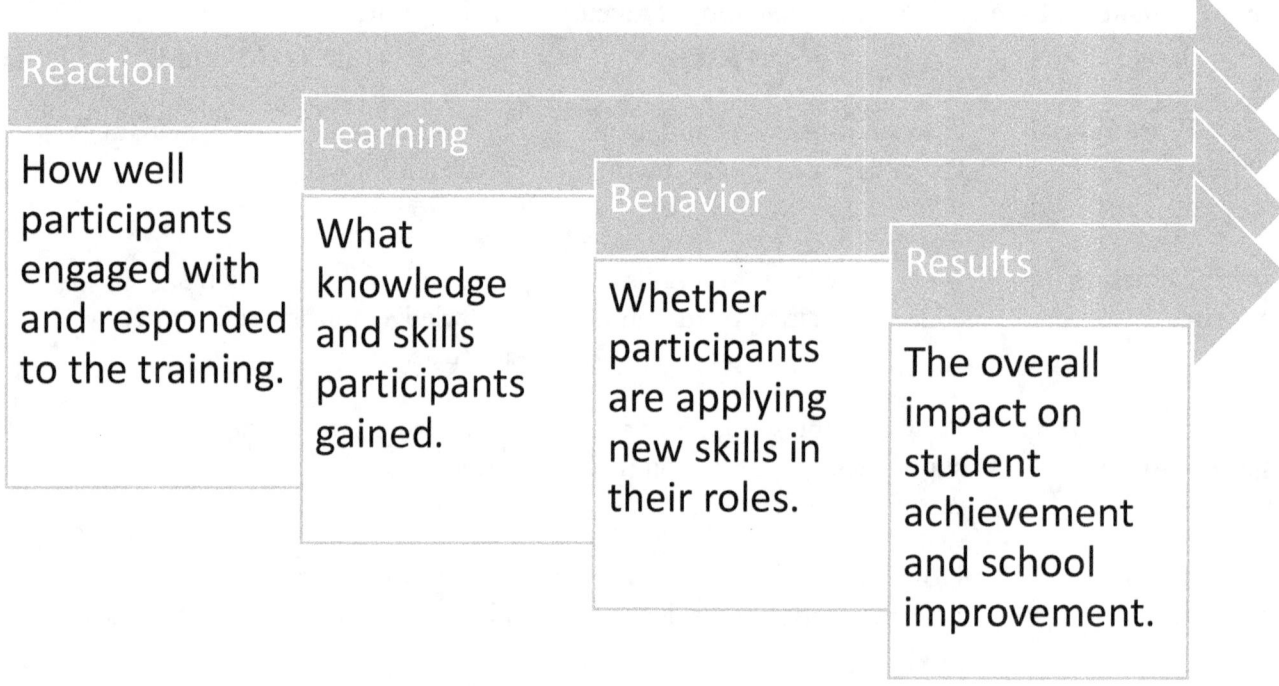

Each level provides deeper insights into whether PD efforts are effective and leading to meaningful changes.

Comparing Guskey's and Kirkpatrick's Models

While both models emphasize evaluating professional learning across multiple levels, they have distinct focuses:

- Guskey's model places greater emphasis on organizational support and student learning outcomes.
- Kirkpatrick's model is widely used in corporate and education settings, with a focus on participant learning and behavior change.

Table 3.2: Comparing Guskey's and Kirkpatrick's PD Evaluation Models

Aspect	Guskey's Model	Kirkpatrick's Model
Focus	Long-term impact on student learning and educator application.	Short-term impact on engagement, learning, and behavior change.
Levels of Evaluation	Five levels, including **organizational support**.	Four levels, with emphasis on **individual application**.
Best Used For	Schools and districts measuring **system-wide implementation**.	Individual teacher training sessions and **small-group PD efforts**.

> **Action Step:** Schools should combine elements of both models to create a comprehensive PD evaluation strategy that assesses immediate engagement, long-term application, and student impact.

Selecting the Right Evaluation Methods for MTSS PD

To effectively assess MTSS professional development, schools must choose evaluation tools that align with their learning goals and implementation timeline.

The table below outlines recommended evaluation tools for different PD outcomes.

Table 3.3: Selecting Evaluation Methods for MTSS Professional Development

Evaluation Focus	Best Evaluation Methods	Example Questions
Participant Satisfaction	Surveys, feedback forms.	*Did the PD meet your expectations? Was the content engaging and relevant?*
Knowledge & Skill Acquisition	Pre/post-assessments, quizzes, reflective journals.	*What are three key takeaways from this session?*
Application of Learning	Classroom observations, fidelity checklists, coaching sessions.	*Are educators consistently implementing MTSS strategies?*
Impact on Student Outcomes	Student progress monitoring, discipline data, academic performance.	*Are students making measurable progress as a result of educator PD?*

> **Action Step:** Schools should use a mix of surveys, assessments, and real-world observations to measure PD impact.

Conclusion

Assessing MTSS professional development requires a structured approach to ensure that training efforts are effective, sustainable, and impactful.

Key takeaways from this section include:

- ✓ **Guskey's model focuses on educator learning, implementation fidelity, and student outcomes.**
- ✓ **Kirkpatrick's model emphasizes engagement, learning, application, and organizational results.**
- ✓ **A combination of surveys, assessments, observations, and student data provides a comprehensive evaluation strategy.**
- ✓ **Schools should select evaluation methods that align with their specific PD goals and timeline.**

By using these models and strategies, schools can ensure that MTSS training efforts lead to real, measurable improvements in educator practice and student success.

The next section will explore key performance indicators (KPIs) for assessing MTSS PD effectiveness, providing a detailed look at what metrics schools should track to measure long-term impact.

Section 3: Key Performance Indicators (KPIs) for Evaluating MTSS Professional Development

Introduction

Effective assessment of MTSS professional development (PD) requires the use of Key Performance Indicators (KPIs)—measurable data points that track progress, effectiveness, and impact. KPIs help schools and districts determine whether MTSS training efforts are leading to meaningful changes in educator practice and student success.

Rather than relying solely on subjective feedback or participation rates, KPIs provide quantifiable evidence of improvement in educator skill acquisition, implementation fidelity, student progress, and overall school performance. This section outlines the most critical KPIs for evaluating MTSS professional development, ensuring that schools can track short-term and long-term outcomes of their training initiatives.

Key Learning Objectives

By the end of this training module, educators and administrators will be able to:

- **Define key performance indicators (KPIs)** in the context of MTSS PD evaluation.
- **Identify critical KPIs** for measuring educator engagement, implementation fidelity, and student outcomes.
- **Use data-driven insights** to assess and refine MTSS training programs.
- **Develop a KPI tracking system** to monitor progress over time.

Defining Key Performance Indicators (KPIs) in MTSS PD

KPIs provide concrete evidence that professional learning is leading to improved instructional practices, effective intervention delivery, and student success.

What Makes a Strong KPI?

- ✓ **Specific:** Clearly defines what is being measured (e.g., percentage of teachers implementing Tier 2 interventions correctly).
- ✓ **Measurable:** Can be tracked with quantifiable data (e.g., student growth percentiles, fidelity check scores).
- ✓ **Actionable:** Provides insight into whether professional development is working or needs adjustments.
- ✓ **Relevant:** Aligns with district goals for MTSS implementation.
- ✓ **Time-Bound:** Includes a timeframe for tracking and evaluating progress.
- ➢ **Action Step:** Schools should select 5-10 core KPIs that align with their MTSS training objectives to monitor professional development effectiveness.

Key Performance Indicators for MTSS Professional Development

The following KPIs are grouped into three primary categories:

1. **Educator Engagement & Participation Metrics**
2. **Implementation Fidelity & Application Metrics**
3. **Student Impact & Outcome Metrics**

1. Educator Engagement & Participation Metrics

Tracking how many educators participate in MTSS training and their level of engagement helps schools determine whether PD opportunities are reaching the right people and meeting their needs.

Critical KPIs for Educator Engagement

KPI	What It Measures	Data Collection Method
PD Attendance Rate	Percentage of educators attending required MTSS training.	Sign-in sheets, LMS (Learning Management System) tracking.
Completion Rate for Online Modules	Percentage of participants who complete online training modules.	LMS analytics, course completion reports.
Educator Satisfaction Score	How educators rate the usefulness and relevance of training.	Post-training surveys (Likert scale ratings).
Self-Reported Confidence Growth	Educators' perceived improvement in understanding and applying MTSS strategies.	Pre- and post-training confidence surveys.

> ➤ **Action Step:** If engagement KPIs are low, schools should adjust training formats, increase incentives, or collect additional feedback to improve accessibility and relevance.

2. Implementation Fidelity & Application Metrics

Participation alone does not indicate PD success. Implementation fidelity KPIs track whether educators are correctly applying MTSS strategies in their daily practice.

Critical KPIs for Implementation Fidelity

KPI	What It Measures	Data Collection Method
Fidelity of Intervention Delivery	Percentage of educators implementing interventions correctly and consistently.	Classroom observations, fidelity checklists.
MTSS Team Meeting Participation	Frequency of educator participation in MTSS problem-solving meetings.	Meeting attendance logs.
Use of Data for Decision-Making	Percentage of teachers using progress monitoring data to adjust instruction.	Teacher surveys, data tracking logs.
Intervention Adherence Score	Consistency in following intervention protocols.	Coaching observations, intervention logs.

> ➤ **Action Step:** If fidelity KPIs are low, schools should increase coaching, provide refresher training, or develop MTSS mentoring programs.

3. Student Impact & Outcome Metrics

The ultimate goal of MTSS professional development is to improve student success through better instruction and intervention. Student-focused KPIs measure whether PD efforts are translating into academic, behavioral, and social-emotional growth.

Critical KPIs for Student Impact

KPI	What It Measures	Data Collection Method
Student Progress Monitoring Growth	Percentage of students meeting growth targets in Tier 2/Tier 3 interventions.	Universal screening and progress monitoring data.
Reduction in Tier 3 Referrals	Decrease in the number of students requiring intensive interventions.	MTSS referral records.
Behavioral Incident Reduction	Decrease in office discipline referrals (ODRs) following PBIS/SEL training.	Behavioral tracking systems, school discipline records.
Academic Achievement Gains	Student improvement in standardized test scores or formative assessments.	State assessments, classroom benchmarks.
Special Education Referral Rates	Whether MTSS training reduces unnecessary referrals to special education.	Special education identification data.

> **Action Step:** If student impact KPIs are not improving, schools should analyze intervention quality, refine PD focus areas, and adjust instructional practices.

Using KPI Dashboards to Track MTSS PD Effectiveness

To streamline data collection and make KPI analysis more efficient, schools should create MTSS PD dashboards that track key metrics in real-time.

Best Practices for KPI Dashboards

- ✓ **Use visual data representation** – Graphs and charts make it easier to interpret progress.
- ✓ **Automate data collection** – Pull data from LMS systems, observation tools, and student performance reports.
- ✓ **Update regularly** – KPI dashboards should be reviewed at least quarterly.
- ✓ **Share findings with stakeholders** – Principals, MTSS teams, and district leaders should use KPI data to refine PD strategies.
- ➢ **Action Step:** Schools should **develop KPI tracking sheets or digital dashboards using Google Sheets, Microsoft Power BI, or district-wide data management platforms.**

Conclusion

Key Performance Indicators (KPIs) provide critical insights into the success of MTSS professional development efforts. By tracking metrics related to educator engagement, implementation fidelity, and student impact, schools can determine what's working and what needs improvement.

Key takeaways from this section include:

- ✓ **Educator engagement KPIs** track participation, satisfaction, and confidence growth.
- ✓ **Implementation fidelity KPIs** measure how well educators are applying MTSS strategies.
- ✓ **Student impact KPIs** assess improvements in academic, behavioral, and social-emotional outcomes.
- ✓ **Data dashboards help visualize trends and guide PD adjustments.**

By consistently monitoring these KPIs, schools can make data-driven decisions to refine MTSS training, ensuring that PD efforts lead to sustained improvements in both educator practice and student success.

The next section will explore feedback collection and continuous improvement strategies, detailing how schools can use educator and student input to enhance MTSS PD over time.

Section 4: Feedback Collection and Continuous Improvement Strategies

Introduction

Effective professional development (PD) for Multi-Tiered System of Supports (MTSS) practitioners is an ongoing process, not a one-time event. To ensure that training efforts remain relevant, effective, and aligned with educator and student needs, schools must implement structured feedback mechanisms and a continuous improvement cycle.

This section explores best practices for collecting educator feedback, analyzing PD effectiveness, and making data-driven adjustments to enhance future training. By incorporating feedback loops and adaptive learning strategies, schools can refine professional development initiatives and sustain long-term MTSS implementation success.

Key Learning Objectives

By the end of this training module, educators and administrators will be able to:

- Use multiple methods to collect educator feedback on MTSS professional development.
- Analyze PD effectiveness using both qualitative and quantitative data.
- Implement a continuous improvement cycle for refining training efforts.
- Encourage a culture of reflective practice and professional growth.

Collecting Meaningful Feedback on MTSS Professional Development

Gathering structured feedback from educators, interventionists, and administrators helps schools determine:

- ✓ What aspects of PD are effective.
- ✓ Where gaps exist in MTSS training.
- ✓ How professional development can be improved.

To ensure comprehensive insights, schools should collect feedback using multiple methods rather than relying on a single survey or discussion.

Best Practices for Gathering Feedback

- ✓ **Collect feedback at different time points** – Gather input immediately after training, and then follow up after implementation to assess long-term effectiveness.
- ✓ **Use a combination of qualitative and quantitative feedback** – Blend survey data, interviews, and observations for a well-rounded perspective.
- ✓ **Encourage honest, constructive responses** – Create anonymous surveys when necessary to allow educators to provide candid feedback.
- ✓ **Ask targeted questions** – Ensure feedback prompts focus on both training content and practical application.
- ➢ **Action Step:** Schools should incorporate structured feedback cycles into all MTSS PD initiatives to ensure continuous program refinement.

Methods for Collecting MTSS PD Feedback

Different feedback collection methods provide unique insights into the effectiveness and impact of MTSS professional development.

Table 3.4: Feedback Collection Methods for MTSS PD

Method	Best Used For	Example Questions
Post-Training Surveys	Immediate participant feedback on training clarity and engagement.	*How relevant was this training to your daily practice? What topics need more depth?*
Focus Groups	In-depth discussions on implementation challenges and PD effectiveness.	*What barriers prevent effective use of MTSS strategies?*
Observation & Coaching Feedback	Assessing real-world application of training concepts.	*Are educators applying new strategies with fidelity?*
Self-Reflection Journals	Encouraging educators to document their learning and growth.	*What was the most valuable takeaway from this PD? How have you applied it in practice?*
Student Outcome Data	Measuring PD effectiveness through student progress.	*Are intervention strategies leading to improved academic/behavioral outcomes?*

> **Action Step:** Schools should implement at least three different feedback methods to capture a comprehensive understanding of PD impact.

Analyzing MTSS Professional Development Effectiveness

Once feedback is collected, schools must analyze the data to identify:

- Strengths of current MTSS training.
- Areas needing improvement or expansion.
- Barriers to implementation fidelity.

Step-by-Step Process for PD Effectiveness Analysis

1. Organize Feedback by Theme

- ❖ Categorize responses into common themes (e.g., **content depth, instructional strategies, training format, implementation challenges**).

2. Compare Educator Feedback with Implementation Data

- ❖ Align participant feedback with **KPIs from Section 3** to determine if **training is translating into effective practice**.

3. Identify Gaps and Trends

- ❖ Look for patterns in feedback—do multiple educators express **the same concerns or requests**?

4. Develop Targeted Adjustments

- ❖ Use insights to **refine future training content, format, or support structures**.
- ➢ **Action Step:** Schools should create summary reports of PD feedback each quarter to track trends and guide decision-making.

Continuous Improvement in MTSS Professional Development

MTSS professional development must be **iterative and responsive**, evolving based on **educator needs, student data, and implementation challenges**.

The Continuous Improvement Cycle for MTSS PD

To ensure long-term effectiveness, schools should implement a **four-step PD improvement cycle**:

Figure 3.3: The MTSS Professional Development Continuous Improvement Cycle

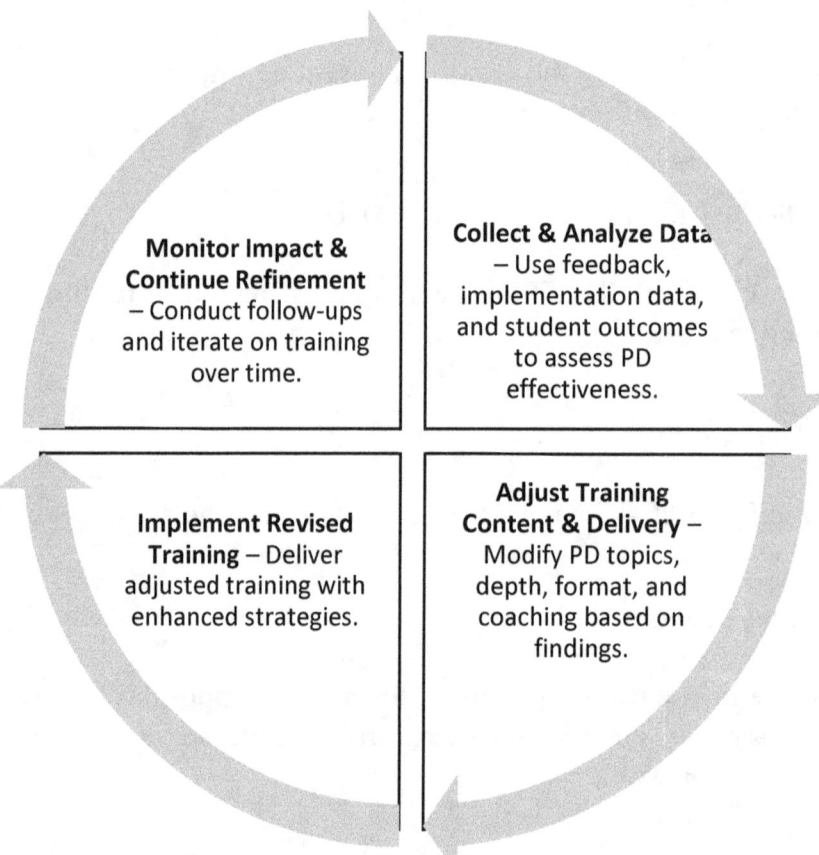

This cycle ensures that MTSS professional learning remains dynamic, effective, and aligned with real-world needs.

Encouraging Reflective Practice and Growth

A culture of reflection is essential for sustained MTSS success. Schools should:

- ✓ **Provide ongoing coaching** – Follow up with educators to discuss PD application and challenges.
- ✓ **Encourage professional learning communities (PLCs)** – Foster peer collaboration for **problem-solving and strategy-sharing**.
- ✓ **Recognize and celebrate successes** – Highlight positive educator growth to maintain engagement and motivation.
- ➢ **Action Step:** Schools should integrate PD reflection sessions into MTSS team meetings to encourage continuous professional learning.

Conclusion

To ensure MTSS professional development leads to real improvements, schools must implement structured feedback loops and a continuous improvement model.

Key takeaways from this section include:

- ✓ **Feedback should be collected using multiple methods**, including surveys, focus groups, and observational data.
- ✓ **PD effectiveness must be analyzed alongside implementation and student outcome data.**
- ✓ **A continuous improvement cycle ensures that professional learning remains relevant and impactful.**
- ✓ **Reflective practice and coaching support long-term educator growth.**

By embedding feedback-driven refinements into MTSS professional learning, schools can maximize the impact of training and ensure that interventions lead to meaningful student success.

The next section will explore case studies of successful MTSS professional development programs, highlighting real-world examples of effective training models and their impact on educator practice and student outcomes.

Section 5: Case Studies of Successful MTSS Professional Development Programs

Introduction

Real-world examples provide valuable insight into what makes MTSS professional development effective. While theoretical models and data-driven assessment strategies are essential, case studies illustrate how these principles are applied in practice to improve educator capacity and student outcomes.

This section highlights successful MTSS professional development initiatives from three different school districts, showcasing their training models, implementation strategies, challenges faced, and measurable results. These case studies offer practical takeaways that schools can adapt and apply to their own MTSS training efforts.

Key Learning Objectives

By the end of this training module, educators and administrators will be able to:

- Examine real-world examples of MTSS professional development programs.
- Identify key factors that contribute to successful MTSS training implementation.
- Analyze common challenges and solutions in professional development efforts.
- Apply best practices from case studies to their own school or district.

Case Study 1: District-Wide MTSS Implementation with Coaching Support

District Profile:

- **Location:** Large suburban school district (15 elementary schools, 5 middle schools, 3 high schools)
- **Student Population:** 42,000 students

- **Challenge:** Inconsistent MTSS implementation across schools due to varying educator knowledge and training gaps
- **Solution:** Year-long professional development series with embedded coaching

Training Model:

- ✓ **Year-long PD series** with **monthly workshops** on MTSS best practices
- ✓ **Job-embedded coaching model** – Each school was assigned an MTSS coach to provide **on-the-ground support**
- ✓ **MTSS Implementation Playbook** – Standardized guidelines for intervention protocols, progress monitoring, and team collaboration

Results:

- ➤ **Increased intervention fidelity** – Observations showed a 40% increase in correct implementation of Tier 2 interventions.
- ➤ **Educator confidence growth** – Post-training surveys showed a 72% improvement in teachers' self-efficacy in using MTSS strategies.
- ➤ **Reduction in Tier 3 referrals** – After two years, Tier 3 referrals dropped by 28%, indicating better support at Tiers 1 and 2.

Key Takeaways:

- ✓ On-site coaching improves implementation fidelity.
- ✓ Standardized training materials create consistency across schools.
- ✓ Ongoing professional learning (not one-time workshops) leads to lasting change.

Case Study 2: Data-Driven MTSS Training for Rural Schools

District Profile:

- **Location:** Rural district with six K-8 schools
- **Student Population:** 4,800 students
- **Challenge:** Limited access to in-person PD due to location and scheduling constraints
- **Solution:** Hybrid professional development model using **virtual training and in-person application**

Training Model:

- ✓ **Virtual MTSS PD modules** – Self-paced online training covering intervention strategies, progress monitoring, and team collaboration
- ✓ **Live Q&A sessions** with MTSS specialists **every two weeks** for real-time support
- ✓ **Data review meetings** – Educators met **monthly** to review student progress data and adjust interventions accordingly

Results:

- ➢ **Higher participation rates – 91% of educators completed the full training series,** compared to 63% in previous years with in-person workshops.
- ➢ **Improved data usage** – Teachers demonstrated **a 60% increase in data-driven decision-making** for interventions.
- ➢ **More targeted Tier 2 support** – The percentage of students **exiting Tier 2 interventions successfully** rose from 45% to 67% within one year.

Key Takeaways:

- ✓ Virtual and hybrid training increases accessibility for rural educators.
- ✓ Regular data review meetings strengthen intervention decision-making.
- ✓ Blending asynchronous learning with live support improves training effectiveness.

Case Study 3: Equity-Focused MTSS PD in an Urban District

District Profile:

- ✪ **Location:** Urban district with 10 elementary schools and 3 high schools
- ✪ **Student Population:** 22,500 students (76% economically disadvantaged, 42% English learners)
- ✪ **Challenge:** Disproportionate referrals of students of color to special education and disciplinary actions
- ✪ **Solution:** Culturally responsive MTSS professional development focusing on **equity-based interventions**

Training Model:

- ✓ **Equity-focused PD workshops** on **implicit bias, culturally responsive instruction, and inclusive intervention strategies**
- ✓ **Restorative practices training** for all teachers and administrators to **reduce reliance on punitive discipline**
- ✓ **Data equity audits** conducted **quarterly** to track MTSS implementation gaps

Results:

- ➤ **Reduction in special education over-identification** – The number of **Black and Latino students referred for special education dropped by 35%** over two years.
- ➤ **Decrease in disciplinary referrals** – Out-of-school suspensions dropped by **42%** due to increased use of restorative practices.
- ➤ **Improved academic performance** – Students receiving culturally responsive Tier 2 interventions showed a **15% increase in reading scores**.

Key Takeaways:

- ✓ Culturally responsive MTSS training reduces systemic disparities.
- ✓ Restorative practices create a more inclusive school climate.
- ✓ Regular equity audits help track progress and refine interventions.

Common Themes and Best Practices from Case Studies

These case studies highlight **several key strategies** that make MTSS professional development effective:

1. Professional Development Must Be Sustained, Not One-Time

- ✖ **Ineffective:** One-time PD workshops with no follow-up.
- ✓ **Effective:** Year-long training series with embedded coaching and ongoing support.

2. Data-Driven Decision-Making Strengthens MTSS Implementation

- ✖ **Ineffective:** Educators using interventions inconsistently or without tracking progress.
- ✓ **Effective:** Regular data review meetings to refine intervention strategies.

3. Equity-Focused Training Improves Outcomes for Diverse Learners

- ✖ **Ineffective:** Using a "one-size-fits-all" intervention model.
- ✓ **Effective:** Providing culturally responsive interventions tailored to student backgrounds.

4. Hybrid and Virtual Training Expands Access to MTSS PD

- ✖ **Ineffective:** Relying solely on in-person workshops, limiting participation.
- ✓ **Effective:** Blending **asynchronous online learning with live Q&A and coaching support**.
- ➤ **Action Step:** Schools should **incorporate at least two of these best practices** into their own MTSS professional development models to improve training effectiveness.

Conclusion

These real-world case studies demonstrate how structured, data-driven, and equity-focused MTSS professional development leads to improved implementation fidelity and better student outcomes.

Key takeaways from this section include:

- ✓ Sustained, year-long training models lead to deeper implementation.
- ✓ Data-driven decision-making improves intervention effectiveness.
- ✓ Equity-based MTSS PD reduces disparities in special education and discipline.
- ✓ Virtual and hybrid PD formats increase accessibility for rural and busy educators.

By applying these evidence-based strategies, schools can strengthen their MTSS training efforts, ensuring educators feel supported and students receive high-quality interventions.

The next chapter will explore designing a district-wide MTSS professional development plan, providing a step-by-step guide for creating structured, scalable, and effective training initiatives at the school or district level.

Chapter 4: Designing a District-Wide MTSS Professional Development Plan

Section 1: Chapter Overview

Introduction to the Chapter's Focus

Scaling Multi-Tiered System of Supports (MTSS) professional development (PD) across an entire district requires careful planning, strategic alignment, and long-term sustainability. While individual schools may implement MTSS training, a district-wide approach ensures consistency, equitable access to resources, and a unified vision for intervention practices.

This chapter provides a step-by-step framework for designing a district-wide MTSS PD plan, covering goal setting, stakeholder involvement, training structures, resource allocation, and evaluation methods. By following this framework, school districts can develop structured, scalable, and effective MTSS training initiatives that lead to long-term improvement in both educator practice and student outcomes.

Key Objectives and Learning Outcomes

By the end of this chapter, readers will be able to:

- Understand the key components of a district-wide MTSS professional development plan.
- Identify critical stakeholders needed for successful implementation.
- Develop a structured, multi-phase PD timeline that aligns with district goals.
- Allocate resources effectively to support MTSS training.
- Create a system for monitoring and sustaining MTSS PD efforts over time.

To provide an overview of **the essential components** of district-wide MTSS PD planning, **Figure 4.1 illustrates the five key pillars** of a successful professional development framework.

Figure 4.1: Five Key Pillars of a District-Wide MTSS PD Plan

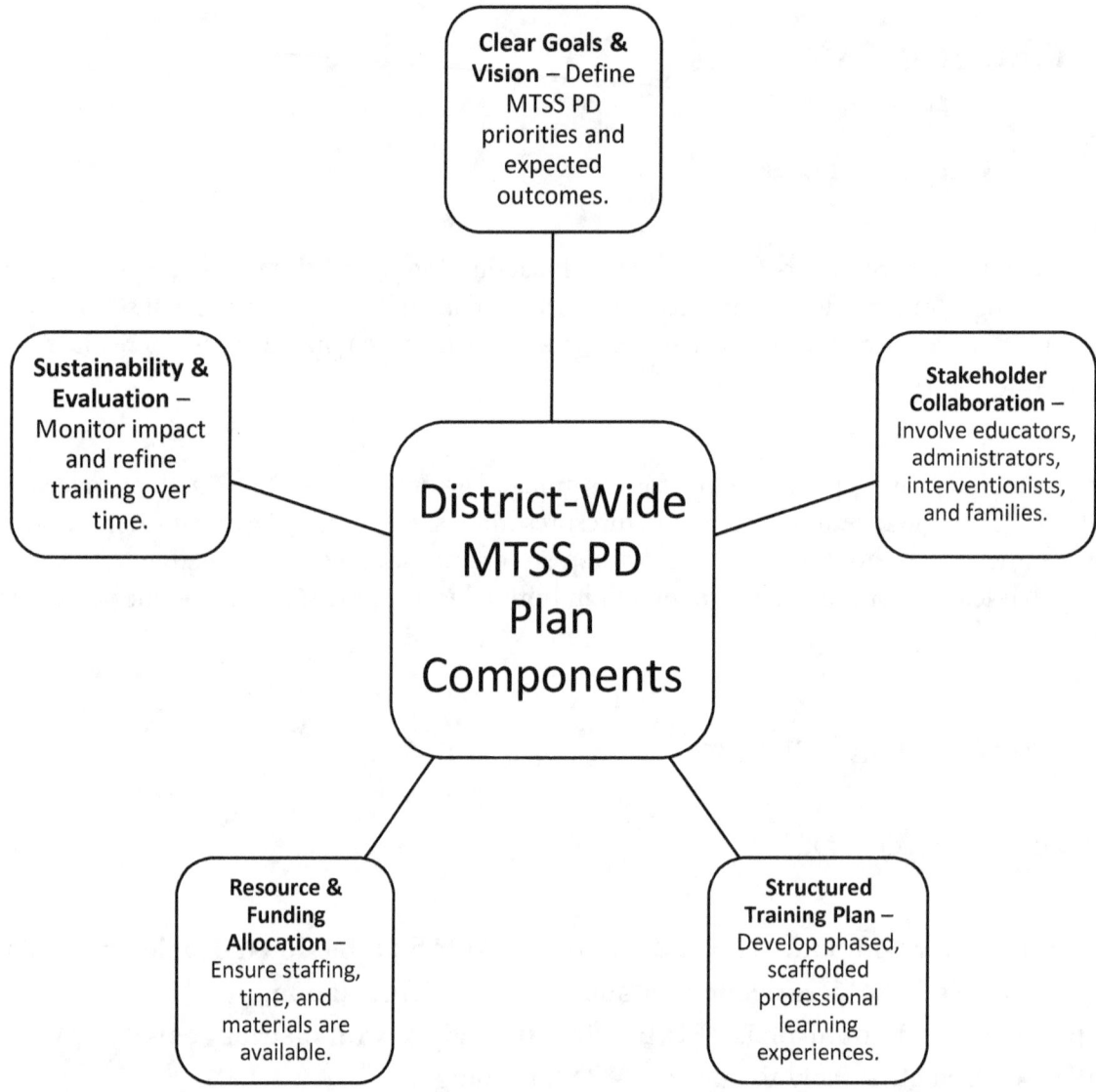

Each of these pillars will be explored in greater depth in the following sections, ensuring that districts can build an effective and scalable MTSS training model that leads to measurable success.

In the next section, we will explore how to establish clear MTSS PD goals and align them with district priorities, ensuring that professional learning is purpose-driven and outcome-oriented.

Section 2: Establishing Clear Goals and Alignment with District Priorities

Introduction

A successful district-wide MTSS professional development (PD) plan must begin with a clear vision and well-defined goals. Without a focused set of priorities, PD efforts risk becoming disjointed, inconsistent, or misaligned with district needs. Schools must ensure that MTSS training initiatives are strategically aligned with broader district objectives, such as improving academic achievement, reducing discipline disparities, and fostering inclusive, data-driven intervention practices.

This section explores how to establish clear, measurable MTSS PD goals, align them with district-wide strategic plans, and create a roadmap for professional learning that supports educators, interventionists, administrators, and student support staff.

Key Learning Objectives

By the end of this training module, educators and administrators will be able to:

- **Define specific, measurable goals for MTSS professional development.**
- **Align MTSS PD with district priorities and continuous improvement initiatives.**
- **Develop a structured MTSS PD vision statement.**
- **Use data to inform professional development planning and goal-setting.**

Defining MTSS Professional Development Goals

Effective PD goals should be clear, actionable, and measurable, ensuring that training efforts directly contribute to improving MTSS implementation fidelity and student outcomes.

Characteristics of Strong MTSS PD Goals

- ✓ **Specific:** Clearly outlines the focus area of professional learning (e.g., increasing educator confidence in Tier 2 intervention delivery).
- ✓ **Measurable:** Includes **concrete success indicators (e.g., 90% of teachers will implement Tier 1 differentiated instruction strategies by the end of the semester).**
- ✓ **Achievable:** Aligned with available resources, staffing, and time constraints.
- ✓ **Relevant:** Supports district-wide MTSS priorities and improvement plans.
- ✓ **Time-Bound:** Includes a clear timeline for implementation and assessment.
- ➢ **Action Step:** Districts should develop 3-5 core goals for MTSS PD, ensuring each goal is aligned with educator needs and student success metrics.

Aligning MTSS Professional Development with District Priorities

MTSS professional development should not function as a standalone initiative—it must integrate with existing district priorities and improvement efforts. Aligning training with broader district goals ensures coherence, stakeholder buy-in, and sustainability.

Examples of Alignment Between MTSS PD and District Priorities

District Priority	Aligned MTSS PD Focus	Example Goal
Improving Early Literacy Outcomes	Training on **evidence-based Tier 1 reading interventions**	85% of K-3 teachers will demonstrate proficiency in structured literacy strategies by the end of the year.
Reducing Discipline Disparities	Training on **restorative practices & culturally responsive PBIS**	Reduce out-of-school suspensions by 25% within two years.
Enhancing Data-Driven Decision Making	PD on **progress monitoring tools and data interpretation**	100% of MTSS teams will conduct monthly data review meetings.
Supporting Special Populations (ELs, SPED)	Training on **inclusive MTSS interventions for diverse learners**	Increase targeted Tier 2/3 EL support by 30% over one year.

- ➢ **Action Step:** Districts should ensure that MTSS PD goals are directly connected to their strategic improvement plans for student achievement, equity, and educator effectiveness.

Developing a District-Wide MTSS PD Vision Statement

A clear and compelling vision statement serves as a guiding force for MTSS training initiatives, ensuring all stakeholders share a common understanding of professional learning priorities.

Key Components of a Strong MTSS PD Vision Statement

- ✓ **Purpose-Driven:** Explains **why** MTSS professional learning matters.
- ✓ **Aspirational Yet Attainable:** Reflects the district's commitment to growth and improvement.
- ✓ **Aligned with Core MTSS Values:** Emphasizes equity, data-driven practices, and continuous learning.
- ✓ **Inclusive of All Stakeholders:** Recognizes the roles of teachers, interventionists, administrators, and support staff.

Example MTSS Professional Development Vision Statement

"Our district is committed to providing high-quality, evidence-based professional development that empowers all educators to implement MTSS with fidelity, ensuring that every student receives personalized, data-driven support to achieve academic and social-emotional success. Through ongoing training, coaching, and collaboration, we strive to build a culture of continuous learning that promotes equity, inclusion, and positive student outcomes."

- ➤ **Action Step:** District leadership should collaborate with **MTSS coordinators, instructional coaches, and educators to develop a shared PD vision statement that aligns with local priorities.**

Using Data to Inform MTSS PD Goal-Setting

Data should drive all MTSS PD planning efforts, ensuring that training priorities are based on actual implementation gaps and student needs.

Key Data Sources for Informing PD Goals

- ✓ **MTSS Fidelity Assessments** – Identify gaps in educator implementation of tiered interventions.
- ✓ **Educator Surveys & Self-Assessments** – Gauge teacher confidence and PD needs.
- ✓ **Student Progress Monitoring Data** – Highlight trends in intervention effectiveness.
- ✓ **Behavior & Discipline Reports** – Reveal areas where behavior interventions need improvement.
- ✓ **Special Education Referral Trends** – Assess whether early intervention efforts are reducing unnecessary referrals.
- ➢ **Action Step:** Districts should conduct annual MTSS data reviews to ensure PD goals are aligned with areas needing improvement.

Conclusion

Establishing clear goals and alignment with district priorities ensures that MTSS professional development is structured, relevant, and results-driven.

Key takeaways from this section include:

- ✓ **MTSS PD goals should be specific, measurable, and time-bound.**
- ✓ **Training efforts must align with district-wide priorities, such as literacy, equity, and data-driven decision-making.**
- ✓ **A strong MTSS PD vision statement unifies stakeholders and reinforces commitment to continuous learning.**
- ✓ **Data should inform all goal-setting efforts** to ensure professional learning addresses real-world challenges in MTSS implementation.

The next section will explore stakeholder collaboration in MTSS PD planning, detailing how to engage educators, administrators, families, and community partners to build a sustainable, district-wide training framework.

Section 3: Stakeholder Collaboration in MTSS PD Planning

Introduction

A district-wide MTSS professional development (PD) plan cannot succeed without the active involvement of key stakeholders. Effective MTSS implementation requires collaboration between teachers, interventionists, administrators, school psychologists, families, and community partners. Without buy-in from these groups, training efforts may be seen as top-down mandates rather than meaningful professional learning opportunities.

This section explores how to engage stakeholders in MTSS PD planning, ensure diverse perspectives are represented, and build collective ownership of professional learning initiatives. By fostering collaboration, districts can create a sustainable training model that is responsive to educator needs and student success.

Key Learning Objectives

By the end of this training module, educators and administrators will be able to:

- **Identify key stakeholder groups essential to MTSS PD planning and implementation.**
- **Develop strategies for engaging teachers, administrators, and support staff in MTSS PD design.**
- **Ensure family and community involvement in MTSS training efforts.**
- **Create collaborative structures that sustain professional learning beyond initial implementation.**

Key Stakeholders in MTSS PD Planning

Each stakeholder group plays a **critical role** in shaping and sustaining effective MTSS professional learning initiatives.

Table 4.1: Key MTSS PD Stakeholders and Their Roles

Stakeholder Group	Role in MTSS PD Planning
Teachers & Interventionists	Provide insight into classroom challenges and PD needs; implement MTSS strategies in daily instruction.
School & District Administrators	Allocate resources, set priorities, and support PD implementation across schools.
Instructional Coaches & MTSS Coordinators	Lead PD sessions, model best practices, and provide job-embedded coaching.
School Psychologists & Counselors	Contribute expertise on behavioral and social-emotional interventions.
Families & Caregivers	Support student learning and reinforcement of MTSS strategies at home.
Community Partners	Provide additional training resources, mentorship programs, and afterschool intervention support.

> **Action Step:** Districts should establish an MTSS PD Planning Committee composed of representatives from each stakeholder group to ensure diverse perspectives are included.

Engaging Educators in MTSS PD Design

Why Teacher Input Matters

Teachers and interventionists are on the front lines of MTSS implementation, making their input invaluable in designing PD that is practical, relevant, and effective. PD that is teacher-informed is more likely to:

- ✓ Address **real classroom challenges**.
- ✓ Be seen as **meaningful and useful**, rather than a compliance requirement.
- ✓ Increase **teacher buy-in and motivation** to implement MTSS strategies.

Best Practices for Teacher Engagement

- ✓ **Conduct Needs Assessments** – Use surveys and focus groups to gather feedback on training gaps and preferred PD formats.
- ✓ **Create Teacher Leadership Roles** – Identify MTSS teacher leaders to co-facilitate PD and serve as peer mentors.
- ✓ **Use a Collaborative PD Model** – Incorporate Professional Learning Communities (PLCs) where teachers can reflect on and refine MTSS implementation.
- ✓ **Provide Choice in PD Topics** – Offer customized training pathways so teachers can select PD sessions that align with their roles (e.g., Tier 1 classroom strategies vs. Tier 2/3 intervention techniques).
- ➤ **Action Step:** Districts should establish MTSS Teacher Advisory Groups to ensure that PD content reflects educator priorities and instructional realities.

The Role of Administrators in MTSS PD Implementation

School and district administrators set the tone for MTSS professional learning. Without their visible support, training efforts may lack accountability and follow-through.

How Administrators Can Support MTSS PD

- ✓ **Model Commitment to MTSS Training** – Actively participate in professional learning alongside educators.
- ✓ **Provide Time for Collaboration** – Ensure that teachers have dedicated time for PD and MTSS team meetings.
- ✓ **Allocate Resources Effectively** – Budget for ongoing training, coaching support, and intervention tools.
- ✓ **Embed MTSS PD into School Improvement Plans** – Align training goals with district-wide academic and behavioral priorities.
- ➤ **Action Step:** District leadership should **integrate MTSS PD expectations into administrator evaluation criteria** to reinforce its importance.

Engaging Families & Community Partners in MTSS Training

Families and community organizations play a crucial role in reinforcing MTSS strategies beyond the school setting. When parents understand how MTSS supports their child's learning and well-being, they become valuable partners in intervention success.

Best Practices for Family & Community Engagement

- ✓ **Offer Parent Workshops on MTSS** – Educate families about tiered supports, intervention processes, and ways to help at home.
- ✓ **Provide Accessible Training Resources** – Share multilingual MTSS guides, videos, and tip sheets to ensure all families can engage.
- ✓ **Partner with Local Organizations** – Work with community centers, libraries, and youth programs to provide extended learning opportunities.
- ✓ **Encourage Two-Way Communication** – Use parent surveys and advisory groups to gather feedback on MTSS training efforts.

Example: Family Engagement Success Story

A district in Texas partnered with local libraries to host family MTSS nights, where parents learned how to support literacy interventions at home. As a result, reading proficiency among Tier 2 students improved by 20% in one year.

- ➤ **Action Step:** Schools should establish Family MTSS Learning Series events to promote parent and caregiver understanding of intervention strategies.

Creating Sustainable Collaborative Structures for MTSS PD

Collaboration should extend beyond initial MTSS training—it must become an embedded part of school culture. Sustainable structures ensure that PD efforts continue evolving and improving over time.

Best Practices for Sustaining MTSS PD Collaboration

- ✓ **Professional Learning Communities (PLCs)** – Regular team meetings where educators share best practices and refine interventions.
- ✓ **MTSS Coaching Networks** – Assign experienced educators as peer coaches to support colleagues.

- ✓ **District MTSS Leadership Teams** – Cross-functional committees that oversee ongoing training efforts and evaluate PD effectiveness.
- ✓ **Annual MTSS Summits** – District-wide conferences where educators share successes, challenges, and innovative intervention strategies.
- ➤ **Action Step:** Schools should embed MTSS collaboration structures into their annual professional learning calendars to ensure sustainability.

Conclusion

Stakeholder collaboration is essential for designing and sustaining effective MTSS professional development. Engaging teachers, administrators, families, and community partners ensures that training efforts are practical, relevant, and widely supported.

Key takeaways from this section include:

- ✓ **MTSS PD planning should involve a diverse range of stakeholders, including teachers, administrators, counselors, and families.**
- ✓ Teachers must have input in PD design to ensure training aligns with real classroom needs.
- ✓ Administrators play a crucial role in supporting MTSS PD through resource allocation and leadership engagement.
- ✓ Families and community organizations should be active partners in reinforcing MTSS strategies.
- ✓ Sustainable collaboration structures—such as PLCs, coaching networks, and leadership teams—help ensure long-term PD success.

By prioritizing stakeholder engagement and collaboration, districts can build an MTSS professional development framework that is high-impact, widely supported, and sustainable over time.

The next section will explore developing a structured, multi-phase professional development timeline, ensuring that training is delivered systematically and strategically throughout the school year.

Section 4: Developing a Structured, Multi-Phase MTSS PD Timeline

Introduction

A successful district-wide MTSS professional development (PD) plan must be implemented strategically over time. If training is delivered in one-time workshops without follow-up, educators may struggle to apply what they have learned, leading to low implementation fidelity and limited impact on student success.

A multi-phase PD timeline ensures that training is:

- ✓ **Scaffolded** – Educators build skills progressively over time.
- ✓ **Job-Embedded** – PD is integrated into daily practice through coaching and collaboration.
- ✓ **Sustainable** – Ongoing learning prevents professional development from becoming **a short-term initiative**.

This section outlines how to structure a year-long MTSS PD plan, ensuring that training is timely, sequential, and aligned with district priorities.

Key Learning Objectives

By the end of this training module, educators and administrators will be able to:

- Develop a structured, multi-phase PD timeline for MTSS training.
- Ensure training progresses from foundational knowledge to advanced implementation.
- Incorporate coaching, collaborative learning, and data-driven refinements throughout the year.
- Align MTSS PD phases with school calendars and district improvement plans.

The Importance of a Multi-Phase PD Approach

Professional development is **most effective when delivered in multiple stages**, allowing educators to **internalize, apply, and refine** their learning over time.

Problems with One-Time Training Sessions

- ✖ **Overwhelming Amount of Information** – Educators receive too much content at once and struggle to retain key concepts.
- ✖ **Lack of Practical Application** – Without structured follow-up, teachers may not integrate MTSS strategies into daily practice.
- ✖ **No Ongoing Support** – Educators need coaching and collaborative reflection to refine their implementation.
- ✖ **Minimal Data-Driven Adjustments** – Without ongoing assessment, PD efforts may not adapt to actual educator needs.

Benefits of a Multi-Phase PD Model

- ✓ **Builds on Prior Learning** – Training moves from introductory concepts to advanced applications.
- ✓ **Provides Time for Application** – Educators can test strategies before receiving further training.
- ✓ **Allows for Data-Driven Adjustments** – Schools can analyze implementation challenges and modify PD accordingly.
- ✓ **Ensures Sustainability** – Educators receive ongoing coaching and collaboration opportunities.
- ➢ **Action Step:** Districts should create a year-long MTSS PD timeline that includes foundational learning, structured application, and ongoing support.

Structuring a Year-Long MTSS PD Timeline

The following four-phase model provides a structured approach to rolling out MTSS professional development over an academic year.

Figure 4.2: Multi-Phase MTSS PD Timeline

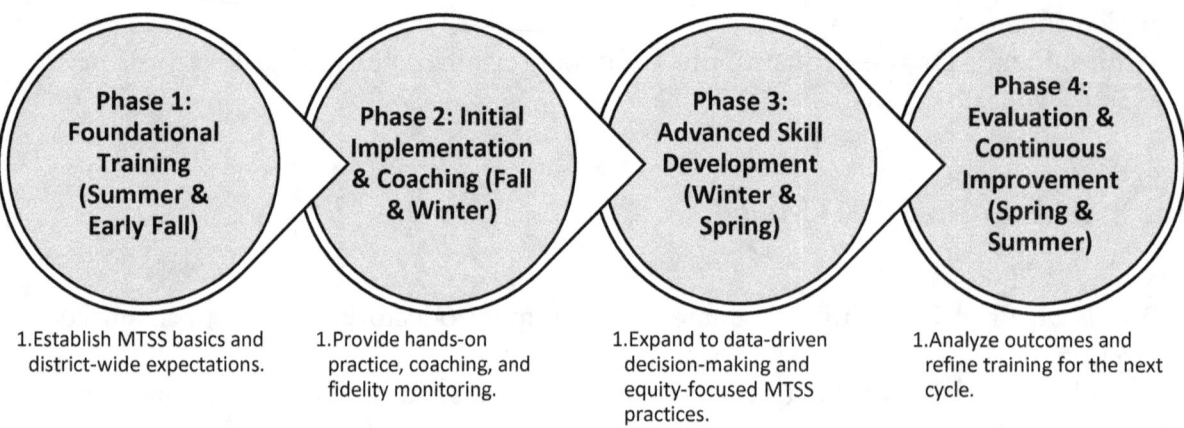

Each phase builds on the previous one, ensuring that MTSS professional learning is progressive and sustainable.

Phase 1: Foundational Training (Summer & Early Fall)

Goal: Build educator knowledge of MTSS principles, tiered interventions, and data-driven decision-making.

Key Activities:

- ✓ **MTSS Kickoff Training** – District-wide workshops covering core MTSS concepts.
- ✓ **Role-Specific Training** – Separate sessions for teachers, interventionists, and administrators to clarify responsibilities.
- ✓ **Data Review & Baseline Assessment** – Schools analyze current MTSS implementation levels and student needs.

- ✓ **Initial Professional Learning Communities (PLCs)** – Establish collaborative teams to discuss challenges and implementation strategies.
- ➢ **Action Step:** Ensure that all educators complete a foundational MTSS training module before the school year begins.

Phase 2: Initial Implementation & Coaching (Fall & Winter)

Goal: Support educators as they begin implementing MTSS strategies, ensuring fidelity and confidence in application.

Key Activities:

- ✓ **Job-Embedded Coaching** – Instructional coaches and MTSS coordinators observe classrooms and provide real-time feedback.
- ✓ **Tiered Intervention Workshops** – Deep dives into Tier 1, Tier 2, and Tier 3 intervention strategies.
- ✓ **Progress Monitoring Training** – Teachers learn how to collect and analyze student data effectively.
- ✓ **Collaborative Problem-Solving Meetings** – Schools hold monthly MTSS team meetings to review data and adjust interventions.
- ➢ **Action Step:** Conduct MTSS fidelity checks during classroom observations to ensure that intervention strategies are being applied correctly.

Phase 3: Advanced Skill Development (Winter & Spring)

Goal: Deepen educators' ability to use data-driven decision-making and equity-focused MTSS practices.

Key Activities:

- ✓ **Equity-Based MTSS Training** – Workshops on culturally responsive teaching, reducing bias in intervention referrals, and restorative practices.
- ✓ **Advanced Data Analysis Workshops** – Educators learn to use student progress data to refine intervention plans.

- ✓ **Intensive Coaching for High-Need Schools** – Additional support for schools with low MTSS implementation fidelity.
- ✓ **Peer Observation & Best Practice Sharing** – Educators visit classrooms to see effective MTSS strategies in action.
- ➤ **Action Step:** Provide MTSS leadership training for teacher leaders and administrators to build long-term capacity for sustaining PD efforts.

Phase 4: Evaluation & Continuous Improvement (Spring & Summer)

Goal: Assess the impact of MTSS PD, refine training content, and plan for the next year.

Key Activities:

- ✓ **Educator Feedback Surveys** – Collect input on what worked well and what needs improvement.
- ✓ **Student Outcome Analysis** – Compare pre- and post-PD intervention effectiveness.
- ✓ **District-Wide MTSS Summit** – Share success stories, celebrate progress, and showcase best practices.
- ✓ **Revise Next Year's PD Plan** – Use feedback and data to improve the next cycle of MTSS training.
- ➤ **Action Step:** Ensure a structured reflection process so that PD improvements are based on real implementation challenges and successes.

Conclusion

A structured, multi-phase MTSS PD timeline ensures that professional learning efforts are progressive, practical, and sustainable.

Key takeaways from this section include:

- ✓ **MTSS training should be scaffolded across four phases:** foundational learning, initial implementation, advanced development, and continuous improvement.
- ✓ **Job-embedded coaching and collaborative PLCs** ensure educators receive support **beyond initial training sessions**.

- ✓ **Data should drive PD decisions**, ensuring training aligns with **actual implementation challenges**.
- ✓ **Regular evaluation and refinement** help **improve PD efforts year over year**.

By implementing a well-planned, phased approach, districts can create a sustainable MTSS professional development model that fosters long-term educator growth and student success.

The next section will explore effective resource and funding allocation strategies to ensure that districts can provide high-quality, ongoing MTSS training without financial strain.

Section 5: Effective Resource and Funding Allocation for MTSS PD

Introduction

Implementing a high-quality, sustainable MTSS professional development (PD) program requires strategic allocation of resources and funding. Without sufficient support, even the most well-designed PD initiatives may fail due to inconsistent implementation, lack of instructional materials, or insufficient coaching support.

Districts must ensure that MTSS PD funding is aligned with training priorities, educator needs, and student success goals. This section explores best practices for securing funding, allocating resources efficiently, and leveraging available grants and partnerships to support ongoing, scalable MTSS training.

Key Learning Objectives

By the end of this training module, educators and administrators will be able to:

- Identify key funding sources for MTSS professional development.
- Allocate resources effectively to sustain long-term MTSS training efforts.
- Leverage grants, partnerships, and alternative funding strategies.
- Create a district-wide budget plan for MTSS PD initiatives.

Key Resources Needed for Effective MTSS PD

To sustain effective MTSS training, districts must allocate resources to support:

- ✓ **Personnel Support** – Hiring MTSS coordinators, instructional coaches, and specialists.
- ✓ **Training & Workshops** – Onsite and virtual training sessions for educators and administrators.
- ✓ **Coaching & Mentoring** – Ongoing job-embedded support to reinforce MTSS strategies.
- ✓ **Technology & Assessment Tools** – Digital platforms for tracking student progress and intervention fidelity.
- ✓ **Instructional Materials** – Research-based curriculum resources for tiered intervention.
- ✓ **Collaboration Time** – Scheduled MTSS team meetings and PLCs for data-driven discussions.
- ➤ **Action Step:** Districts should conduct a resource audit to assess gaps in MTSS implementation and determine funding priorities.

Funding Sources for MTSS Professional Development

Districts can use multiple funding streams to support MTSS PD, combining federal, state, and local resources to ensure sustainability.

Table 4.2: Key Funding Sources for MTSS PD

Funding Source	Description	Best Used For
Title I Funds	Federal funding for schools serving economically disadvantaged students.	MTSS training for Tier 1 interventions, coaching support.
Title II Funds	Federal funding for educator professional learning.	Teacher training, coaching, and leadership development.
IDEA Funds	Supports students with disabilities through individualized interventions.	Special education-focused MTSS training and supports.
ESSER Grants	Emergency federal funding for school recovery.	Expanding MTSS PD efforts, purchasing intervention materials.
State PD Grants	State-based grants for educator training and instructional improvement.	Targeted MTSS coaching and PLC initiatives.
Local District Budgets	General funds allocated for school improvement.	Ongoing PD implementation and intervention resources.

> ➤ **Action Step:** District leaders should review federal and state grant eligibility criteria annually to ensure they are maximizing available funding for MTSS training.

Allocating Resources Effectively

To maximize impact, districts must prioritize funding allocations based on MTSS implementation goals and areas of greatest need.

Best Practices for Resource Allocation

- ✓ **Prioritize Job-Embedded Coaching:** Allocate funding for MTSS specialists or instructional coaches to provide ongoing support.
- ✓ **Invest in Digital Assessment Tools:** Ensure educators have access to universal screeners and progress monitoring platforms.
- ✓ **Fund Tiered Intervention Materials:** Purchase evidence-based instructional resources for Tiers 1, 2, and 3.
- ✓ **Schedule Dedicated Collaboration Time:** Provide funding for MTSS team meetings and professional learning communities (PLCs).
- ✓ **Leverage Partnerships for Cost Savings:** Collaborate with universities, regional education centers, and professional organizations to reduce training costs.
- ➤ **Action Step:** Districts should develop an annual MTSS PD budget plan that aligns financial resources with training priorities.

Leveraging Grants, Partnerships, and Cost-Effective Strategies

1. Applying for Federal & State Grants

Many states offer MTSS-specific grant opportunities that can be used for:

- ✓ Professional learning for educators.
- ✓ Expanding intervention programs.
- ✓ Developing leadership capacity in MTSS implementation.

Example: A district in North Carolina secured a state innovation grant to fund MTSS coaching support in high-need schools, leading to a 30% increase in Tier 2 intervention effectiveness.

- ➤ **Action Step:** Schools should designate a grant-writing team to identify and apply for state and federal funding opportunities.

2. Partnering with Universities & Educational Organizations

Higher education institutions and professional organizations often provide:

- ✓ **Low-cost training programs** for MTSS implementation.
- ✓ **Research-based instructional strategies** aligned with best practices.
- ✓ **Graduate courses** that count toward professional learning credits.

Example: A district partnered with a local university's education department to provide free professional development workshops on culturally responsive MTSS strategies.

> **Action Step:** Districts should establish **formal partnerships with local universities** to access **affordable or grant-funded PD programs**.

---

3. Using Cost-Effective PD Models

Districts can reduce training **costs** by implementing:

- ✓ **Hybrid PD Models** – Blend asynchronous online training with in-person coaching.
- ✓ **Train-the-Trainer Programs** – Identify MTSS teacher leaders to lead PD sessions instead of hiring external consultants.
- ✓ **Peer Mentorship Networks** – Create coaching cohorts where experienced educators support colleagues.

Example: A school district in Illinois implemented a train-the-trainer MTSS model, leading to a 50% reduction in PD costs while increasing educator participation.

> **Action Step:** Schools should adopt cost-efficient training structures, such as peer-led workshops and online learning modules, to maximize their budget.
>

Developing a District-Wide MTSS PD Budget Plan

To ensure sustainability, districts must develop a structured budget plan that aligns funding with PD priorities.

Key Components of an MTSS PD Budget Plan

- ✓ **Annual Funding Breakdown:** List of anticipated expenses and available funding sources.
- ✓ **Resource Prioritization Plan:** Identifies high-need areas (e.g., coaching support, technology upgrades).
- ✓ **Grant Application Strategy:** Timeline for securing external funding.
- ✓ **Cost-Efficiency Measures:** Strategies to reduce training costs while maintaining effectiveness.
- ✓ **Monitoring & Accountability Plan:** Process for tracking spending and adjusting allocations as needed.
- ➤ **Action Step:** Districts should conduct annual budget reviews to ensure financial sustainability of MTSS PD initiatives.

Conclusion

Strategic resource and funding allocation are critical for sustaining district-wide MTSS professional development efforts. Without dedicated financial planning, training initiatives may become fragmented, underfunded, or short-lived.

Key takeaways from this section include:

- ✓ **Multiple funding sources (Title I, II, IDEA, ESSER, state grants) can support MTSS PD efforts.**
- ✓ **Resources should be prioritized for coaching, technology, and intervention materials.**
- ✓ **Grants and university partnerships can significantly reduce training costs.**
- ✓ **Cost-effective PD models (hybrid learning, train-the-trainer programs) maximize budget efficiency.**
- ✓ **Developing a structured MTSS PD budget plan ensures long-term sustainability.**

By strategically aligning funding with professional development goals, districts can ensure that MTSS training efforts are effective, scalable, and sustainable.

The next section will explore monitoring and sustaining MTSS professional development efforts, ensuring that training remains impactful over time through ongoing assessment and refinement.

Section 6: Monitoring and Sustaining MTSS Professional Development Efforts

Introduction

Implementing a district-wide MTSS professional development (PD) plan is only the beginning. To ensure long-term impact, districts must establish systems for monitoring effectiveness, refining training based on data, and sustaining professional learning over time.

Without structured monitoring and continuous improvement efforts, MTSS PD can become stagnant, leading to low implementation fidelity, lack of educator engagement, and minimal impact on student outcomes.

This section explores best practices for tracking MTSS PD success, using data to refine training, and ensuring sustainability through ongoing coaching, professional learning communities (PLCs), and leadership support.

Key Learning Objectives

By the end of this training module, educators and administrators will be able to:

- **Develop systems for monitoring the effectiveness of MTSS professional development.**
- **Use data to refine and improve ongoing MTSS training efforts.**
- **Sustain professional learning through coaching, PLCs, and leadership engagement.**
- **Create a long-term professional development sustainability plan.**

Monitoring the Effectiveness of MTSS Professional Development

Why Monitoring Matters

✖ Without ongoing monitoring:

- Educators may struggle to apply MTSS strategies effectively.

- Training may not address real-world challenges faced in schools.
- Districts cannot determine if PD investments are leading to student improvement.

✓ **With ongoing monitoring:**

- Schools can identify which PD strategies are working and which need refinement.
- Educators receive targeted support based on implementation challenges.
- District leaders can adjust training content and formats to maximize impact.

> **Action Step:** Districts should develop a monitoring framework that includes data collection, feedback loops, and targeted follow-up support.

Key Metrics for MTSS PD Monitoring

Districts must use a mix of quantitative and qualitative data to assess the effectiveness of MTSS professional development.

Table 4.3: Key MTSS PD Monitoring Metrics

Metric Category	Key Indicators	Data Collection Methods
Educator Engagement & Training Completion	PD participation rates, module completion percentages.	Attendance logs, LMS tracking.
Implementation Fidelity	% of teachers correctly implementing MTSS interventions.	Classroom observations, fidelity checklists.
Impact on Student Outcomes	Student growth in academic, behavioral, and SEL interventions.	Progress monitoring data, assessment scores.
Educator Confidence & Preparedness	% of teachers reporting confidence in MTSS implementation.	Pre/post-training surveys, focus groups.
Collaboration & Support	Frequency of PLC meetings and coaching sessions.	Meeting logs, coaching reports.

> **Action Step:** Districts should establish a data collection schedule to assess MTSS PD effectiveness at least quarterly.

Using Data to Refine and Improve MTSS PD

Once data is collected, districts must use it to make informed decisions about improving training efforts.

Best Practices for Using MTSS PD Data

- ✓ **Analyze Trends Over Time** – Compare data before and after training to measure progress.
- ✓ **Use Feedback to Adjust Training** – Modify PD content based on teacher-reported challenges.
- ✓ **Identify Schools Needing Additional Support** – Provide extra coaching for schools struggling with MTSS implementation.
- ✓ **Share Success Stories** – Highlight effective strategies and educator improvements to maintain momentum.
  - > **Action Step:** District leaders should hold quarterly MTSS PD review meetings to analyze data and adjust training plans.

Sustaining Professional Learning Over Time

One-time training is not enough to sustain high-quality MTSS implementation. Districts must embed continuous professional learning structures to keep educators engaged and growing in their MTSS practice.

1. Embedding Coaching & Mentorship

Job-embedded coaching is one of the most effective ways to sustain MTSS training.

- ✓ **Instructional coaches** should work alongside teachers, providing real-time feedback and support.
- ✓ **Mentorship programs** can pair experienced MTSS educators with newer teachers for peer coaching.
- ✓ **Regular check-ins** ensure that educators are not left to implement MTSS strategies in isolation.
- > **Action Step:** Districts should allocate funding for dedicated MTSS instructional coaches or train lead teachers as peer mentors.

2. Leveraging Professional Learning Communities (PLCs)

PLCs create ongoing collaboration opportunities, allowing educators to:

- ✓ **Discuss MTSS challenges and successes.**
- ✓ **Analyze student data and refine interventions.**
- ✓ **Share best practices and implementation strategies.**

Example: A district in Colorado established monthly MTSS PLCs, leading to a 25% improvement in intervention fidelity within one year.

- ➤ **Action Step:** Schools should schedule at least one dedicated PLC session per month focused on MTSS implementation and problem-solving.

3. Building Leadership Support & Accountability

MTSS professional development efforts are only sustainable if district and school leaders remain committed.

How Administrators Can Support MTSS PD Sustainability

- ✓ **Model Participation** – School leaders should attend MTSS training and PLCs.
- ✓ **Provide Incentives** – Recognize educators who excel in MTSS implementation.
- ✓ **Ensure MTSS Is a Priority** – Embed MTSS into school improvement plans and administrator evaluations.
- ✓ **Allocate Ongoing Funding** – Secure annual budget allocations for MTSS training and coaching.
- ➤ **Action Step:** District leadership should conduct annual MTSS implementation reviews to maintain focus and accountability.

Developing a Long-Term MTSS PD Sustainability Plan

To ensure that professional learning efforts do not fade over time, districts must develop a structured sustainability plan.

Key Components of an MTSS PD Sustainability Plan

- ✓ **Multi-Year Training Roadmap** – Outline a 3- to 5-year plan for PD progression.
- ✓ **Built-In Review Cycles** – Conduct annual evaluations to refine training based on data.
- ✓ **Designated MTSS Champions** – Train teacher leaders and administrators to sustain MTSS efforts.
- ✓ **Institutionalized PLCs & Coaching** – Ensure that collaborative learning structures are permanent.
- ➢ **Action Step:** Districts should integrate MTSS PD sustainability planning into their annual strategic planning process.

Conclusion

Sustaining effective MTSS professional development requires ongoing monitoring, data-driven refinement, and embedded professional learning structures.

Key takeaways from this section include:

- ✓ **MTSS PD should be continuously monitored using implementation fidelity and student outcome data.**
- ✓ **Data should inform PD refinements, ensuring training remains responsive to educator needs.**
- ✓ Sustainable PD structures include job-embedded coaching, PLCs, and leadership accountability.
- ✓ Long-term MTSS PD sustainability plans ensure professional learning efforts do not fade over time.

By embedding a culture of continuous learning and refinement, districts can ensure that MTSS professional development leads to lasting improvements in educator practice and student success.

The next chapter will provide a comprehensive case study of a district that successfully implemented a sustainable, high-impact MTSS professional development model, offering practical insights and lessons learned.

Chapter 5: Case Study – Implementing a Sustainable, High-Impact MTSS Professional Development Model

Section 1: Chapter Overview

Introduction to the Chapter's Focus

This chapter provides a real-world case study of a school district that successfully implemented a sustainable, high-impact Multi-Tiered System of Supports (MTSS) professional development (PD) model. By examining this case, readers will gain practical insights into the challenges, solutions, and outcomes of scaling MTSS training across a district.

The case study highlights the district's phased approach to professional learning, key stakeholder collaboration, and use of data-driven decision-making to sustain high-quality MTSS implementation. Readers will also explore lessons learned and best practices that can be applied in their own districts.

Key Objectives and Learning Outcomes

By the end of this chapter, readers will be able to:

- **Examine real-world challenges and solutions** related to implementing district-wide MTSS professional development.
- **Identify best practices for phased implementation, coaching support, and collaborative learning.**
- Understand how data-driven decision-making supports sustained MTSS PD success.
- Apply lessons learned from the case study to their own district's training efforts.

District Profile and Context

- **District Name:** River Valley Unified School District (RVUSD)
- **Location:** Mid-sized suburban district in the Midwest
- **Student Population:** Approximately 18,500 students across 22 schools
- **Demographics:** 42% economically disadvantaged, 30% English learners, 14% students with disabilities

Initial Challenges:

1. Inconsistent MTSS implementation across schools.
2. Low intervention fidelity and minimal data-driven decision-making.
3. Disproportionate special education and discipline referrals for marginalized student groups.
4. Lack of ongoing coaching and support for teachers and interventionists.

Key Phases of Implementation

River Valley Unified School District implemented a three-phase MTSS professional development model over three years. Each phase was designed to address specific implementation challenges and progressively build educator capacity.

Phase 1: Building a Strong Foundation (Year 1)

Focus:

- ✓ Establishing district-wide MTSS training.
- ✓ Clarifying roles and responsibilities.
- ✓ Creating a unified data system for tracking student progress.

Key Strategies:

- Conducted district-wide MTSS kickoff training for all educators and administrators.
- Developed an MTSS Playbook, outlining intervention protocols and data collection procedures.
- Provided job-embedded coaching for high-need schools.

Results:

- ➤ 95% of educators completed foundational MTSS training.
- ➤ Progress monitoring data was standardized across all schools.
- ➤ Initial fidelity assessments showed a 20% increase in Tier 1 intervention consistency.

Phase 2: Expanding Coaching Support and Collaborative Learning (Year 2)

Focus:

- ✓ Strengthening job-embedded support.
- ✓ Expanding professional learning communities (PLCs).
- ✓ Using data to refine intervention strategies.

Key Strategies:

- Assigned full-time MTSS coaches to each school cluster.
- Established monthly PLCs focused on data analysis and intervention problem-solving.
- Provided advanced training on culturally responsive interventions and restorative practices.

Results:

- ➤ PLC attendance increased to 88% across all schools.
- ➤ Fidelity assessments showed a 35% improvement in Tier 2 implementation accuracy.
- ➤ Out-of-school suspensions decreased by 30%, due to increased use of restorative practices.

Phase 3: Sustaining and Scaling Success (Year 3)

Focus:

- ✓ Embedding MTSS into school culture and leadership practices.
- ✓ Establishing long-term sustainability structures.
- ✓ Celebrating success and sharing best practices.
- ✓

Key Strategies:

- Integrated MTSS implementation reviews into school improvement plans.
- Held an annual MTSS Best Practices Summit, where educators shared success stories.
- Created peer mentorship networks to support new teachers and interventionists.

Results:

- 100% of schools included MTSS goals in their annual improvement plans.
- Student reading proficiency improved by 12% district-wide.
- Special education referral rates for marginalized student groups decreased by 28%.

Key Challenges and Solutions

Challenge	Solution
Resistance to change among some educators.	Provided **teacher-led PD sessions** and peer mentorship opportunities.
Lack of time for data review meetings.	Allocated **dedicated PLC time** during professional development days.
High turnover among MTSS coaches.	Developed **succession plans** and provided **leadership training** for future coaches.
Limited funding for ongoing training.	Secured **state equity grants** and partnered with **local universities** to offer low-cost PD.

Best Practices from the Case Study

The following best practices emerged from River Valley Unified School District's MTSS PD model:

- ✓ **Phased Implementation:** Training efforts were rolled out **progressively over three years**, allowing for **refinement and scalability**.
- ✓ **Job-Embedded Coaching:** Full-time coaches provided **ongoing, real-time support** for teachers and administrators.
- ✓ **Data-Driven Refinement:** Educators used **progress monitoring and fidelity assessments** to adjust interventions.
- ✓ **Collaborative Learning:** Monthly PLCs provided a space for **peer support and shared problem-solving**.
- ✓ **Leadership Engagement:** District and school leaders **actively participated in training** and held educators accountable for implementation.

Lessons Learned

1. **Sustained support is essential:** One-time training sessions are ineffective without follow-up coaching and collaboration opportunities.
2. **Data must drive decision-making:** Schools must use multiple data sources to monitor progress and refine training.
3. **Equity-focused practices reduce disparities:** Culturally responsive interventions and restorative practices led to significant improvements in student outcomes.
4. **Teacher leadership increases buy-in:** Teachers were more engaged in PD when peer leaders facilitated sessions.
5. **Flexibility is key:** The district adapted its training plan based on feedback and implementation challenges.

Conclusion

This case study demonstrates that a phased, data-driven approach to MTSS professional development can lead to sustained improvements in both educator practice and student success.

Key takeaways from this chapter include:

- ✓ **Progressive implementation allows for refinement and scalability.**
- ✓ **Job-embedded coaching and collaborative learning structures** sustain professional growth.
- ✓ **Data-driven decision-making ensures that training aligns with real-world challenges.**
- ✓ **Leadership engagement and accountability** are critical for long-term success.
- ✓ **Equity-focused practices** reduce systemic disparities and improve outcomes for marginalized students.

By applying these best practices and lessons learned, districts can develop high-impact MTSS training models that lead to lasting improvements in school performance and student success.

The next chapter will provide practical guidelines and templates for creating district-wide MTSS professional development plans, ensuring that readers can apply the insights gained from previous chapters to their own schools and districts.

Section 2: Practical Guidelines for Replicating the Model in Other Districts

Introduction

The success of River Valley Unified School District's (RVUSD) MTSS professional development (PD) model provides a proven framework that other districts can adapt to their unique contexts. However, replicating an MTSS PD model requires intentional planning, alignment with local needs, and ongoing adaptation based on data and feedback.

This section outlines practical steps, templates, and tools to help other districts develop a customized, scalable MTSS PD model that ensures sustainable educator growth and student success.

Key Learning Objectives

By the end of this training module, readers will be able to:

- Adapt RVUSD's phased MTSS PD model to their district's needs.
- Develop a step-by-step action plan for professional learning implementation.
- Use templates and tools to streamline planning, tracking, and evaluation.
- Ensure sustainability through coaching, leadership support, and data-driven refinement.

Step 1: Conduct a Readiness Assessment

Before launching an MTSS PD model, districts must assess their current capacity, educator needs, and system-wide implementation gaps.

Key Readiness Indicators

- ✓ **MTSS Implementation Fidelity:** Do schools follow tiered intervention guidelines consistently?
- ✓ **Educator Knowledge Gaps:** What aspects of MTSS require the most training (e.g., data use, intervention delivery, SEL integration)?
- ✓ **Existing PD Structures:** Does the district have coaching, PLCs, and data review systems in place?
- ✓ **Stakeholder Buy-In:** Are administrators, teachers, and support staff committed to MTSS training efforts?
- ✓ **Funding Availability:** What federal, state, and local resources can support professional learning?
- ➢ **Action Step:** Districts should conduct an MTSS PD Readiness Survey to gather educator feedback and baseline data before designing a training plan.

Step 2: Develop a Phased MTSS PD Implementation Plan

To ensure scalability and sustainability, districts should structure MTSS PD across three progressive phases, following the River Valley model.

Table 5.1: Recommended Phases for Implementing MTSS PD

Phase	Focus Area	Key Strategies	Timeframe
Phase 1: Building Foundations	Introduce MTSS principles and align district expectations.	District-wide training, role-specific workshops, initial fidelity checks.	Year 1, Fall-Spring
Phase 2: Strengthening Implementation	Support educators in applying interventions and using data effectively.	Job-embedded coaching, PLCs, leadership engagement, progress monitoring.	Year 2, Ongoing
Phase 3: Sustaining & Scaling	Institutionalize best practices for long-term MTSS success.	Peer mentorship, annual MTSS summits, continuous improvement plans.	Year 3+

➤ **Action Step:** District leaders should create a phased MTSS PD roadmap that aligns with their local school calendars and improvement plans.

Step 3: Assign MTSS Leadership Roles & Responsibilities

To ensure smooth implementation, districts must establish clear leadership roles for overseeing MTSS PD efforts.

Table 5.2: MTSS PD Leadership Roles

Role	Responsibilities
MTSS Director	Oversees district-wide MTSS implementation and professional development.
MTSS Coaches	Provide real-time instructional support, model best practices, and ensure intervention fidelity.
School-Based MTSS Teams	Lead data review meetings, support teachers, and monitor implementation.
Teacher Leaders	Facilitate PLCs, mentor colleagues, and share best practices.

➤ **Action Step:** Districts should designate MTSS PD leadership teams in each school and provide them with additional training to support their peers.

Step 4: Embed Coaching & Collaborative Learning Structures

To sustain professional growth, districts must integrate coaching and peer collaboration into MTSS PD.

Best Practices for Sustaining MTSS Learning

- ✓ **Job-Embedded Coaching:** Assign MTSS specialists to work alongside educators.
- ✓ **Professional Learning Communities (PLCs):** Create monthly MTSS data meetings for intervention adjustments.
- ✓ **Peer Mentorship Programs:** Pair experienced teachers with new educators to strengthen MTSS skills.
- ✓ **Online Learning Modules:** Offer on-demand training to provide flexibility in professional learning.
- ➤ **Action Step:** Schools should schedule dedicated MTSS collaboration time within staff meeting structures or early-release PD days.

Step 5: Create an MTSS PD Tracking & Accountability System

To measure MTSS PD effectiveness, districts must track:

- ✓ **PD participation rates** and engagement levels.
- ✓ **Implementation fidelity of tiered interventions.**
- ✓ **Student progress and intervention effectiveness.**

Table 5.3: MTSS PD Data Collection Methods

Metric	Data Source	Review Frequency
PD Attendance	Sign-in sheets, LMS tracking	Monthly
Educator Confidence & Readiness	Pre/post-training surveys	Semesterly
Fidelity of Intervention Implementation	Classroom observations, coaching logs	Quarterly
Student Academic Growth	Progress monitoring assessments	Every 6-8 weeks

> **Action Step:** Districts should develop an MTSS PD dashboard to track training effectiveness and refine strategies based on data.

Step 6: Sustain MTSS PD Through Long-Term Planning

Strategies for Long-Term MTSS PD Success

- ✓ **Develop a multi-year training roadmap** to align professional learning with district goals.
- ✓ **Secure ongoing funding** through Title I, II, IDEA, and state grants.
- ✓ **Institutionalize PLCs and coaching structures** to embed MTSS into daily practice.
- ✓ **Recognize and celebrate progress** to maintain momentum and educator engagement.
- ✓ **Ensure leadership continuity** by training new administrators and teacher leaders in MTSS implementation.
- > **Action Step:** Districts should incorporate MTSS professional learning sustainability into their school improvement plans to ensure ongoing commitment and accountability.

Conclusion

By following a structured, multi-phase approach, districts can successfully replicate the River Valley MTSS PD model while adapting it to their specific needs.

Key takeaways from this section include:

- ✓ **Districts must conduct a readiness assessment before launching MTSS PD initiatives.**
- ✓ **A phased approach to MTSS PD ensures gradual, scalable implementation.**
- ✓ **Clear leadership roles and coaching support sustain professional learning.**
- ✓ **Collaborative learning structures (PLCs, coaching, mentorship) reinforce educator growth.**
- ✓ **Tracking data and refining PD based on feedback lead to long-term success.**

By integrating these best practices, districts can build an effective and sustainable MTSS training model that ensures consistent intervention implementation, educator confidence, and improved student outcomes.

The next section will provide customizable templates and planning tools to support districts in designing their MTSS professional development initiatives, ensuring efficient planning and execution of training efforts.

Section 3: Customizable Templates and Planning Tools for MTSS PD Implementation

Introduction

Successfully implementing a district-wide MTSS professional development (PD) model requires strategic planning, documentation, and progress tracking. To support districts in replicating an effective and scalable MTSS PD framework, this section provides customizable templates and planning tools for each phase of professional learning.

These tools will help district leaders, MTSS coordinators, and instructional coaches design, implement, and monitor structured, data-driven training initiatives that align with their district's educator needs and student achievement goals.

Key Learning Objectives

By the end of this training module, educators and administrators will be able to:

- Use planning templates to structure district-wide MTSS PD efforts.
- Develop customized training roadmaps, coaching schedules, and data tracking tools.
- Implement fidelity checklists to ensure high-quality intervention delivery.
- Monitor and adjust MTSS PD initiatives using progress assessment forms.

Essential MTSS PD Planning Templates and Tools

The following customizable templates provide structured support for MTSS PD implementation. Each tool is designed to be adaptable to different district contexts and can be used digitally or in print format.

1. MTSS Professional Development Planning Template

This template provides a high-level overview of an MTSS PD plan, ensuring alignment with district priorities, available resources, and training objectives.

Table 5.4: MTSS PD Planning Template

Category	Details to Include
District Goals	What district-wide MTSS priorities will this PD initiative support?
Training Objectives	What skills and knowledge should educators gain from this training?
Target Audience	Who will receive training (teachers, administrators, interventionists)?
Training Formats	Will training be in-person, virtual, asynchronous, or hybrid?
Coaching & Support	How will ongoing coaching and mentorship be incorporated?
Assessment Measures	How will PD effectiveness be tracked and refined?

➤ **Action Step:** Districts should complete this planning template before launching an MTSS PD initiative to ensure alignment with broader goals.

2. MTSS Training Roadmap Template

A training roadmap ensures sequential, scaffolded learning experiences over time. This tool helps districts structure training across phases of implementation.

Table 5.5: MTSS Training Roadmap (Sample Format)

Phase	Focus Area	Key Training Topics	Timeframe
Phase 1	Building Foundations	MTSS Core Principles, Tiered Interventions, Data-Based Decision-Making	August-October
Phase 2	Strengthening Implementation	Fidelity Monitoring, Differentiation Strategies, Equity-Based MTSS Practices	November-February
Phase 3	Sustaining & Scaling	Peer Coaching, Data Deep Dives, Refining MTSS Systems	March-June

➤ **Action Step:** Districts should tailor the training roadmap to their specific school calendar and educator needs.

3. MTSS Coaching & Support Schedule Template

Coaching is a crucial component of sustaining MTSS PD efforts. This template helps districts assign coaching roles and track instructional support efforts.

Table 5.6: MTSS Coaching & Support Schedule

School	Assigned Coach	Coaching Focus	Frequency of Visits
Lincoln Elementary	Jane Smith	Tier 1 Differentiation Strategies	Weekly
West Middle School	Mark Johnson	Data-Driven Decision-Making	Biweekly
East High School	Sarah Adams	Intensive Tier 2 & 3 Support	Monthly

> **Action Step:** Schools should schedule regular coaching visits and ensure that coaches provide structured feedback and implementation support.

4. MTSS Implementation Fidelity Checklist

To ensure that educators correctly apply intervention strategies, districts must conduct fidelity checks using a structured observation form.

Table 5.7: MTSS Implementation Fidelity Checklist

Implementation Area	Observation Criteria	Rating (1-4)	Comments/Next Steps
Tier 1 Instruction	Are teachers using differentiation and universal supports?		
Tier 2 Interventions	Are small-group interventions aligned with student needs?		
Progress Monitoring	Are educators collecting and using data to adjust instruction?		
Collaboration	Are MTSS teams meeting regularly to discuss student needs?		

> **Action Step:** Districts should conduct fidelity checks quarterly to assess MTSS implementation quality and identify areas for PD improvement.

5. MTSS PD Evaluation & Feedback Form

To refine professional learning efforts, districts must gather ongoing feedback from educators. This survey allows teachers to share insights on training effectiveness and suggest improvements.

Table 5.8: MTSS PD Evaluation Form (Sample Questions)

Survey Question	Response Scale (1-5)	Open-Ended Comments
The training content was relevant and applicable to my teaching.		
I feel more confident in implementing MTSS interventions.		
The coaching and PLC sessions were helpful.		
What additional support do you need to implement MTSS effectively?	N/A	

> **Action Step:** Schools should distribute PD feedback surveys after each training session and use responses to refine future sessions.

How to Use These Templates for Maximum Impact

Best Practices for Implementing MTSS PD Planning Tools

- ✓ **Customize Templates for Local Contexts:** Adapt each form to reflect district-specific MTSS goals and challenges.
- ✓ **Embed Tracking Systems:** Store digital versions of these tools in Google Drive, Microsoft Teams, or district PD platforms for easy access.
- ✓ **Ensure Accountability:** Assign specific leaders and coaches to oversee implementation progress.
- ✓ **Review & Adjust Regularly:** Use PD feedback forms and fidelity checklists to refine training throughout the school year.
- ➤ **Action Step:** Districts should create a centralized repository where all MTSS PD planning tools and templates are stored for continuous reference.

Conclusion

By using structured planning templates and tracking tools, districts can streamline MTSS professional development efforts and ensure that training is data-driven, sustainable, and impactful.

Key takeaways from this section include:

- ✓ **Planning templates help align MTSS PD with district goals and training needs.**
- ✓ **A structured training roadmap ensures that professional learning is progressive and scaffolded.**
- ✓ **Coaching schedules, fidelity checklists, and feedback forms provide structured monitoring and accountability.**
- ✓ **Regular evaluation and refinement of MTSS PD efforts ensure sustained success.**

By integrating these customizable templates into their MTSS professional development planning, districts can increase efficiency, improve intervention fidelity, and enhance student outcomes.

The next chapter will explore final recommendations for ensuring district-wide MTSS PD success, summarizing key strategies and providing an action plan for implementation.

Chapter 6: Final Recommendations for Ensuring District-Wide MTSS PD Success

Section 1: Chapter Overview

Introduction to the Chapter's Focus

Implementing and sustaining an effective Multi-Tiered System of Supports (MTSS) professional development (PD) model requires strategic planning, continuous monitoring, and leadership commitment. This chapter synthesizes key insights from previous chapters and provides a final action plan for ensuring long-term success in district-wide MTSS training.

Districts that have successfully built sustainable, high-impact MTSS PD models share common features, including:

- ✓ Clear alignment with district goals and student needs.
- ✓ A phased, data-driven approach to professional learning.
- ✓ Structured coaching and collaboration opportunities.
- ✓ Ongoing assessment and refinement of training initiatives.
- ✓ Strong leadership engagement and stakeholder support.

This chapter will outline best practices, common pitfalls to avoid, and an actionable roadmap for districts seeking to maximize the impact of their MTSS PD efforts.

Key Objectives and Learning Outcomes

By the end of this chapter, readers will be able to:

- Apply final recommendations for building and sustaining MTSS PD.
- Identify and address common challenges in MTSS training efforts.
- Develop a district-wide action plan for professional learning implementation.
- Ensure long-term sustainability through strategic leadership and resource allocation.

Final Best Practices for Successful MTSS Professional Development

1. Align Training with District Priorities and Student Needs

MTSS PD should not operate in isolation—it must be fully aligned with broader district priorities to ensure system-wide impact.

- ✓ **Link MTSS PD to District Improvement Plans:** Training efforts should be explicitly connected to district-wide goals for student achievement, equity, and behavioral support.
- ✓ **Use Data to Drive Training Priorities:** Districts should analyze educator readiness, intervention effectiveness, and student progress data to identify training gaps and high-priority PD areas.
- ✓ **Ensure Role-Specific Training:** Teachers, administrators, interventionists, and support staff should receive differentiated training based on their responsibilities in MTSS implementation.
- ➢ **Action Step:** District leaders should review school improvement plans annually and align MTSS training goals with district-wide performance indicators.

2. Implement a Phased, Scalable Approach to Professional Development

One of the most common mistakes in MTSS training is trying to cover too much at once. A structured, multi-phase PD timeline ensures that training is manageable, scaffolded, and sustainable over time.

Recommended MTSS PD Phases

Phase	Focus Area	Timeframe
Phase 1: Foundational Learning	Introduce MTSS principles, intervention strategies, and data systems.	Year 1: Fall-Spring
Phase 2: Practical Application & Coaching	Provide hands-on support, fidelity checks, and job-embedded coaching.	Year 2: Ongoing
Phase 3: Refinement & Scaling	Institutionalize best practices, peer mentorship, and leadership training.	Year 3+

- ➢ **Action Step:** Districts should use the MTSS Training Roadmap Template (from Chapter 5) to structure professional learning progression across multiple years.

3. Embed Ongoing Coaching and Collaborative Learning Structures

One-time workshops are insufficient for sustaining MTSS implementation. Districts must embed coaching and collaborative structures to reinforce learning.

- ✓ **Designate MTSS Coaches:** Assign instructional specialists or teacher leaders to provide ongoing classroom-based coaching.
- ✓ **Leverage Professional Learning Communities (PLCs):** Ensure monthly PLC meetings focus on MTSS implementation challenges, intervention refinements, and data analysis.
- ✓ **Create Peer Mentorship Networks:** Pair experienced educators with new teachers to strengthen long-term MTSS capacity.
- ➤ **Action Step:** Districts should formalize coaching roles and PLC meeting schedules in their professional development plans.

4. Use Data to Track PD Impact and Adjust Training Strategies

To ensure professional development translates into improved practice and student outcomes, districts must collect and analyze key training metrics.

Table 6.1: Key MTSS PD Metrics and Data Sources

Metric	Data Source	Review Frequency
PD Participation Rates	Attendance logs, LMS tracking	Monthly
Implementation Fidelity	Classroom observations, coaching logs	Quarterly
Educator Confidence & Readiness	Pre/post-training surveys	Semesterly
Student Intervention Effectiveness	Progress monitoring assessments	Every 6-8 weeks

- ➤ **Action Step:** Districts should establish an MTSS PD Data Dashboard to track progress and identify areas for refinement.

5. Ensure Leadership Commitment and Long-Term Sustainability

MTSS professional learning must be a district priority supported by superintendents, principals, and instructional leaders.

- ✓ **Model Active Participation:** Leaders should attend MTSS training sessions and PLC meetings to reinforce commitment.
- ✓ **Allocate Annual Funding:** Ensure **consistent budgeting** for MTSS training, coaching, and resources.
- ✓ **Embed MTSS PD in Leadership Development:** Provide administrator training on supporting MTSS at the school level.
- ➢ **Action Step:** Districts should integrate MTSS PD expectations into administrator evaluations to ensure ongoing leadership accountability.

Common Pitfalls to Avoid in MTSS PD Implementation

Table 6.2: Common Challenges and Solutions in MTSS Training

Common Pitfall	Solution
PD is delivered as a one-time event	Use a **multi-phase training model** with embedded coaching and collaboration.
Educators feel overwhelmed by training expectations	Differentiate PD based on **roles, experience levels, and intervention needs**.
Lack of follow-through after training sessions	Schedule **regular coaching visits, PLC discussions, and fidelity checks**.
Limited stakeholder buy-in	Involve **teachers, administrators, and support staff** in PD planning and decision-making.
No data tracking system in place	Use **PD surveys, implementation checklists, and student progress data** to adjust training.

- ➢ **Action Step:** Districts should review this checklist annually to identify and address potential roadblocks in MTSS PD execution.

District-Wide Action Plan for MTSS Professional Development

To ensure successful and sustainable MTSS PD implementation, districts should develop a structured action plan that aligns with their vision, training needs, and resource availability.

Table 6.3: MTSS PD Action Plan Template

Action Step	Responsible Party	Timeline	Success Indicators
Conduct MTSS Readiness Assessment	District MTSS Coordinator	Summer	Baseline data collected
Develop Multi-Year Training Roadmap	MTSS Leadership Team	Fall	Clear PD phases outlined
Establish Coaching & PLC Structures	School-Based MTSS Teams	Ongoing	Coaching logs, PLC attendance
Implement Data Monitoring System	Instructional Coaches, Principals	Quarterly	Progress monitoring reports
Evaluate & Refine MTSS PD Plan	District Leaders	Annually	PD survey results, student progress trends

> **Action Step:** Districts should use this action plan template to ensure systematic planning, execution, and assessment of their MTSS PD efforts.

Conclusion

Ensuring district-wide success in MTSS professional development requires structured planning, continuous monitoring, and strong leadership commitment.

Key takeaways from this chapter include:

- ✓ Aligning training with district priorities and educator needs ensures impact.
- ✓ A phased, scalable PD approach prevents information overload and supports gradual implementation.
- ✓ Coaching, PLCs, and mentorship programs sustain MTSS learning over time.
- ✓ Data tracking and feedback-driven refinement improve professional learning effectiveness.
- ✓ Leadership commitment and resource allocation ensure MTSS PD remains a priority.

By following these final recommendations and action steps, districts can establish a sustainable, high-impact MTSS training model that leads to lasting improvements in educator practice and student success.

The next section will provide closing remarks and a call to action, encouraging districts to commit to continuous improvement and innovation in MTSS professional learning.

Section 2: Closing Remarks and Call to Action

Introduction

As districts work toward establishing sustainable, high-impact Multi-Tiered System of Supports (MTSS) professional development (PD), it is crucial to embrace continuous improvement, stakeholder collaboration, and data-driven refinement. MTSS professional learning is not a one-time event, but rather an ongoing journey that requires adaptation, persistence, and commitment to student success.

This final section serves as a call to action for district leaders, educators, and stakeholders to remain engaged in refining, scaling, and sustaining their MTSS PD efforts. It outlines the next steps needed to move forward, ensuring that the strategies presented in this book are applied effectively and lead to long-term improvements in both educator practice and student outcomes.

Key Takeaways from the Book

Throughout this book, we have explored the essential components of effective MTSS professional development, including:

- ✓ **Establishing clear goals and alignment with district priorities** to ensure PD efforts drive measurable improvements.
- ✓ **Implementing a structured, phased approach** to professional learning, allowing educators to progressively build capacity.
- ✓ **Embedding coaching and collaborative learning structures**, such as job-embedded coaching, Professional Learning Communities (PLCs), and peer mentorship.
- ✓ **Using data to refine training efforts**, ensuring professional learning remains responsive to educator needs and student progress.
- ✓ **Securing leadership commitment and sustainable funding** to maintain long-term professional learning initiatives.

- **Action Step:** Districts should review their current MTSS PD model and identify which best practices they have successfully implemented and which require further development.

Next Steps for District Leaders and Educators

1. Conduct a District-Wide MTSS PD Audit

Before moving forward, districts must assess the current state of their MTSS professional learning initiatives by conducting an MTSS PD audit. This assessment should include:

- ✓ **Educator Self-Assessment Surveys:** Gathering teacher feedback on PD effectiveness, implementation challenges, and additional support needed.
- ✓ **Fidelity Checks on MTSS Implementation:** Ensuring interventions are delivered as intended and with consistency.
- ✓ **Data Analysis of Student Outcomes:** Identifying gaps in intervention effectiveness and areas for instructional improvement.
- ✓ **Review of PD Participation Rates:** Evaluating which training formats are most engaging and effective for educators.
- ➢ **Action Step:** Districts should schedule an MTSS PD review meeting with key stakeholders at least twice per year to analyze audit findings and adjust training plans.

2. Establish a Long-Term MTSS PD Vision and Sustainability Plan

To ensure continuity and long-term success, districts must embed MTSS PD into their broader school improvement plans.

Key Elements of an MTSS PD Sustainability Plan

- ✓ **Multi-Year Professional Learning Roadmap:** A 3-5 year plan that ensures training remains progressive and scalable.
- ✓ **Ongoing Coaching and PLC Structures:** Dedicated time and personnel to support continued educator development.
- ✓ **Leadership Development Pathways:** Training principals, instructional coaches, and MTSS specialists to sustain the work.
- ✓ **Annual PD Effectiveness Reviews:** Data-driven assessments to adjust and refine training based on educator and student needs.

- ➢ **Action Step:** Districts should develop a formal MTSS PD sustainability plan and share it with stakeholders to maintain long-term accountability.

3. Foster a Culture of Continuous Improvement and Innovation

MTSS professional learning must evolve as new research, instructional strategies, and student needs emerge. Districts should:

- ✓ **Encourage Educator-Led Professional Development:** Identify teacher leaders to facilitate training and share best practices.
- ✓ **Create Regional MTSS Learning Networks:** Partner with neighboring districts, universities, and education agencies to expand knowledge-sharing.
- ✓ **Invest in Digital Learning and Micro-Credentialing: Offer flexible, competency-based PD opportunities** that allow educators to deepen their expertise at their own pace.
- ✓ **Pilot New Training Models and Gather Feedback:** Continuously test, refine, and improve professional learning based on educator and student data.
- ➢ **Action Step:** Districts should allocate time each year for innovation planning, allowing educators to explore new ideas, pilot strategies, and refine MTSS implementation.

A Call to Action: Committing to Effective and Sustainable MTSS Professional Development

The impact of a well-designed MTSS professional learning model extends far beyond professional growth—it directly influences student achievement, equity, and school-wide success.

A Message to District Leaders:

- ❖ Your leadership sets the tone for success. By committing to a data-driven, collaborative, and ongoing MTSS training approach, you empower educators to provide high-quality, targeted interventions that help every student thrive.

A Message to Educators:

- ❖ Your expertise and dedication are the foundation of MTSS success. By actively engaging in training, coaching, and collaborative learning, you strengthen your ability to differentiate instruction, analyze student progress, and implement research-based interventions that make a difference.

A Message to Stakeholders and Policymakers:

- ❖ Your support ensures sustainability. By investing in MTSS professional development, you contribute to a school system where educators are equipped with the tools they need to create inclusive, responsive learning environments for all students.

Final Action Step: Districts should hold an annual MTSS Professional Development Summit to:

- ✓ Reflect on successes and lessons learned.
- ✓ Recognize educators for their contributions.
- ✓ Refine and improve training initiatives for the next school year.

Final Words: The Path Forward

The journey to building and sustaining effective MTSS professional development requires:

- ✓ **Commitment to a long-term vision.**
- ✓ **Collaboration across all levels of the school system.**
- ✓ **Data-driven decision-making and continuous refinement.**
- ✓ **A culture of learning, innovation, and shared accountability.**

As educators, administrators, and district leaders, you have the power to shape the future of MTSS professional learning, ensuring that every teacher is prepared, every intervention is effective, and every student has access to the support they need to succeed.

By implementing the strategies outlined in this book and maintaining a commitment to continuous improvement, your district can build an MTSS professional development model that drives real, lasting change in both educator practice and student success.

Now is the time to take action. Let's build an MTSS professional learning system that empowers educators and transforms student outcomes—one training, one classroom, and one success story at a time.

Glossary of Key Terms

This glossary provides definitions for key terms related to Multi-Tiered System of Supports (MTSS) professional development, ensuring clarity for educators, administrators, and MTSS practitioners.

A

- **Accountability Measures** – Data-driven systems used to ensure educators are implementing MTSS strategies effectively and consistently.
- **Action Plan** – A structured roadmap outlining the steps needed to implement and sustain MTSS professional development initiatives.
- **Asynchronous Learning** – A flexible professional development format where educators complete training independently, often through online modules or recorded sessions.

B

- **Behavioral Interventions** – Targeted strategies used within MTSS to support students' social-emotional and behavioral needs, often implemented in Tier 2 and Tier 3 supports.
- **Blended Learning** – A professional development model that combines in-person and online training methods to provide flexibility for educators.
- **Buy-In** – The level of commitment and support from educators, administrators, and stakeholders in implementing MTSS practices and professional learning initiatives.

C

- **Coaching Model** – A job-embedded approach to professional development where MTSS coaches or instructional leaders provide ongoing support, feedback, and modeling for educators.
- **Collaboration Time** – Dedicated time for educators to engage in professional discussions, typically through **Professional Learning Communities (PLCs)** or MTSS team meetings.
- **Continuous Improvement Cycle** – An iterative process where **schools plan, implement, assess, and refine** MTSS strategies based on data and feedback.

D

- **Data-Based Decision-Making (DBDM)** – The practice of using student performance data to guide instructional planning and intervention strategies within the MTSS framework.

- **Differentiated Instruction** – An approach where educators adjust their teaching methods, content, and assessment to meet the diverse needs of students.
- **District-Wide MTSS PD Plan** – A structured professional development framework designed to provide ongoing, scalable, and sustainable MTSS training for all educators in a district.

E

- **Early Intervention** – Proactive strategies that provide support before academic or behavioral difficulties escalate, often at the Tier 1 or Tier 2 levels.
- **Equity-Based MTSS** – Ensuring that MTSS practices address systemic disparities and provide culturally responsive support for all students.
- **Evidence-Based Practices (EBPs)** – Instructional and intervention strategies backed by research that have been proven effective in improving student outcomes.

F

- **Fidelity of Implementation** – The degree to which educators consistently and accurately apply MTSS practices as intended.
- **Formative Assessment** – Ongoing assessments used to monitor student progress and adjust instructional strategies accordingly.

G

- **Growth Mindset** – A belief that educators and students can continuously improve skills and performance through effort, persistence, and learning.
- **Guided Practice** – An instructional approach where teachers provide structured support as students or educators learn new strategies, gradually shifting responsibility to independent application.

I

- **Implementation Science** – The study of how evidence-based practices are effectively introduced, adopted, and sustained in educational settings.
- **Individualized Education Program (IEP)** – A legal document outlining special education services for students with disabilities; MTSS can help prevent unnecessary referrals by providing early intervention.
- **Intervention Fidelity Checklist** – A tool used to assess whether educators are implementing interventions correctly and consistently within MTSS.

J

- **Job-Embedded Professional Development** – Ongoing training and coaching that takes place within educators' daily work environment, such as in classrooms or PLC meetings.

K

- **Key Performance Indicators (KPIs)** – Measurable data points that track the success of MTSS training efforts, such as educator participation, intervention fidelity, and student progress.

L

- **Leadership Development Pathway** – A professional learning track that **prepares principals, instructional coaches, and teacher leaders** to sustain MTSS initiatives.
- **Learning Walks** – Informal classroom visits where administrators or coaches observe teaching practices and provide non-evaluative feedback.

M

- **Mentorship Program** – A professional development structure where experienced educators provide guidance and support to teachers new to MTSS implementation.
- **Micro-Credentialing** – A competency-based professional learning model where educators earn badges or certifications for completing targeted MTSS training.
- **Multi-Tiered System of Supports (MTSS)** – A comprehensive framework for providing academic, behavioral, and social-emotional support to students through tiered interventions and data-driven decision-making.

P

- **Peer Observation** – A collaborative PD strategy where educators observe and learn from their colleagues' instructional practices in real time.
- **Professional Learning Communities (PLCs)** – Structured, collaborative groups where educators discuss best practices, analyze data, and refine MTSS strategies.
- **Progress Monitoring** – Regular assessment of student progress to determine if interventions are effective and whether adjustments are needed.

R

- **Restorative Practices** – Strategies used in MTSS to build relationships, address conflicts, and reduce exclusionary discipline practices.

- **Rubric for MTSS PD Evaluation** – A scoring tool used to assess the effectiveness of professional development training based on educator feedback, implementation fidelity, and student impact.

S

- **Scaffolded Learning** – A teaching and training method that gradually increases educator responsibility, moving from guided instruction to independent practice.
- **Specially Designed Instruction (SDI)** – Tailored teaching strategies used in special education that can also inform MTSS interventions.
- **Stakeholder Engagement** – The involvement of educators, administrators, families, and community members in shaping and sustaining MTSS training initiatives.
- **Summative Assessment** – An evaluation of student learning at the end of an instructional period, used to measure the effectiveness of Tier 1, 2, or 3 interventions.

T

- **Tier 1 Instruction** – High-quality, research-based instruction provided to all students in the general education setting.
- **Tier 2 Interventions** – Targeted support for students who need additional academic or behavioral assistance beyond Tier 1 instruction.
- **Tier 3 Interventions** – Intensive, individualized interventions for students with significant learning or behavioral challenges.
- **Train-the-Trainer Model** – A PD approach where selected educators receive advanced training and then lead professional learning for their colleagues.

U

- **Universal Screening** – A proactive assessment used to **identify students at risk for academic or behavioral challenges**, helping determine who needs **Tier 2 or Tier 3 interventions**.

V

- **Virtual Professional Development (VPD)** – Online training sessions, webinars, or asynchronous learning opportunities that provide flexibility for educators to engage in MTSS training.

W

- **Wraparound Services** – A holistic approach in MTSS that connects students with academic, behavioral, and community-based supports to address their unique needs.

Conclusion

This glossary serves as a quick reference guide for understanding key MTSS and professional development terms. By familiarizing themselves with these concepts, educators and administrators can more effectively implement, monitor, and sustain high-quality MTSS professional learning initiatives.

- ➤ Action Step: Districts should distribute this glossary to all educators and MTSS teams as part of their professional development resources to ensure consistent language and understanding across schools.

Scholarly References

Below is a list of scholarly references to support the research-based strategies, frameworks, and best practices discussed in this book. These sources provide empirical evidence on MTSS, professional development, coaching, and data-driven decision-making in education.

Multi-Tiered System of Supports (MTSS) & Intervention Effectiveness

1. Burns, M. K., Jimerson, S. R., & VanDerHeyden, A. M. (Eds.). (2016). *Handbook of response to intervention: The science and practice of multi-tiered systems of support* (2nd ed.). Springer.

    - Comprehensive guide on MTSS, response to intervention (RTI), and best practices for intervention delivery.
2. Fuchs, D., & Fuchs, L. S. (2017). Critique of the National Evaluation of RTI: A case for simpler frameworks. *Exceptional Children, 83*(3), 255–268. https://doi.org/10.1177/0014402917693580

    - Discusses the effectiveness of RTI within MTSS and recommends data-driven refinements for intervention practices.
3. McIntosh, K., Goodman, S., & Bohanan, H. (2019). *Integrated multi-tiered systems of support: Blending RTI and PBIS*. Guilford Press.

    - Explores how schools can integrate academic and behavioral interventions within MTSS for improved student outcomes.
4. Sugai, G., & Horner, R. (2020). Sustaining effective multi-tiered systems of support: The critical role of district leadership. *Journal of Positive Behavior Interventions, 22*(4), 197–208. https://doi.org/10.1177/1098300720917815

    - Examines how district leaders influence the success and sustainability of MTSS implementation.

Professional Development & Educator Capacity Building

5. Darling-Hammond, L., Hyler, M. E., & Gardner, M. (2017). *Effective teacher professional development*. Learning Policy Institute.

- Identifies research-based components of effective professional development, emphasizing coaching, collaboration, and active learning.
6. Desimone, L. M., & Garet, M. S. (2015). Best practices in teacher's professional development in the United States. *Psychology, Society, & Education, 7*(3), 252–263. https://doi.org/10.25115/psye.v7i3.515

    - Discusses evidence-based strategies for effective PD, including sustained coaching and data-driven adjustments.
7. Guskey, T. R. (2021). *Evaluating professional learning: Bringing research and best practices into focus.* Corwin.

    - Presents a five-level evaluation model for assessing professional development effectiveness in improving instructional practices.
8. Yoon, K. S., Duncan, T., Lee, S. W. Y., Scarloss, B., & Shapley, K. (2020). *Reviewing the evidence on how teacher professional development affects student achievement.* Institute of Education Sciences.

    - Analyzes the correlation between PD quality and student academic gains.

Coaching & Job-Embedded Professional Learning

9. Kraft, M. A., Blazar, D., & Hogan, D. (2018). The effect of teacher coaching on instruction and achievement: A meta-analysis of the causal evidence. *Review of Educational Research, 88*(4), 547–588. https://doi.org/10.3102/0034654318759268

    - Reviews the impact of instructional coaching on improving teacher practices and student learning outcomes.
10. Knight, J. (2019). *The impact cycle: What instructional coaches should do to foster powerful improvements in teaching.* Corwin.

- Provides a research-based framework for coaching and professional learning in schools.
11. Neumerski, C. M., & Bryk, A. S. (2021). Coaching for sustainable professional learning: Lessons from improvement science. *American Educational Research Journal, 58*(2), 287–322. https://doi.org/10.3102/0002831220980114
- Explores how coaching supports long-term instructional change and sustainability.

Data-Driven Decision Making & MTSS Fidelity Monitoring

12. Hamilton, L., Halverson, R., Jackson, S., Mandinach, E., Supovitz, J., & Wayman, J. (2016). *Using student achievement data to support instructional decision making* (IES Practice Guide). U.S. Department of Education.
- Examines how schools can use student progress monitoring to refine MTSS interventions and instruction.
13. VanDerHeyden, A. M., Witt, J. C., & Gilbertson, D. (2018). Multi-year evaluation of academic screening and progress monitoring. *School Psychology Review, 47*(2), 142–162. https://doi.org/10.17105/SPR-2018-0045.V47-2
- Discusses best practices for using student data to adjust instruction and ensure MTSS intervention fidelity.
14. Gersten, R., Compton, D., Connor, C. M., Dimino, J., Santoro, L., Linan-Thompson, S., & Tilly, W. D. (2020). Assisting students struggling with reading: Response to intervention and multi-tier intervention for reading in the primary grades (Practice Guide). *Institute of Education Sciences*.
- Reviews best practices for monitoring MTSS interventions and adjusting instruction based on progress data.

Equity and Culturally Responsive MTSS Practices

15. Hammond, Z. (2015). *Culturally responsive teaching and the brain: Promoting authentic engagement and rigor among culturally and linguistically diverse students*. Corwin.
- Discusses how MTSS can be adapted to meet the needs of diverse learners through culturally responsive practices.
16. Gay, G. (2018). *Culturally responsive teaching: Theory, research, and practice* (3rd ed.). Teachers College Press.
- Provides evidence-based strategies for ensuring MTSS interventions are inclusive and equity-driven.
17. Skiba, R. J., Artiles, A. J., Kozleski, E. B., Losen, D. J., & Harry, B. (2016). Risks and consequences of oversimplifying educational inequities: A response to Morgan et al. *Educational Researcher, 45*(3), 173–182. https://doi.org/10.3102/0013189X16644606
- Examines how data analysis within MTSS can prevent disproportionate special education referrals.

Sustaining MTSS Professional Development & Scaling Impact

18. Fullan, M. (2020). *Leading in a culture of change* (2nd ed.). Jossey-Bass.
- Discusses leadership strategies for sustaining large-scale educational change, including MTSS implementation.

19. Fixsen, D. L., Naoom, S. F., Blase, K. A., Friedman, R. M., & Wallace, F. (2019). *Implementation research: A synthesis of the literature*. National Implementation Research Network.
- Analyzes the science of implementation and how MTSS professional learning can be effectively sustained in schools.
20. Hattie, J. (2017). *Visible learning for teachers: Maximizing impact on learning*. Routledge.
- Highlights high-impact instructional strategies and how professional learning can improve educator effectiveness.

Conclusion

These scholarly references provide a solid foundation for understanding MTSS, professional development, instructional coaching, and data-driven decision-making. Educators and administrators are encouraged to explore these sources for deeper insights into designing effective, research-based MTSS professional learning initiatives.

Additional Scholarly References

Specialized References for MTSS Professional Development

Below are additional scholarly references in specialized areas, including behavioral interventions, technology-enhanced professional development (PD), and MTSS for special education. These sources further support research-based strategies for sustainable, high-impact MTSS professional learning.

Behavioral Interventions & Social-Emotional Learning (SEL) in MTSS

1. Positive Behavioral Interventions and Supports (PBIS) and MTSS

21. Bradshaw, C. P., Pas, E. T., Debnam, K., & Johnson, S. (2021). Examining the effects of school-wide positive behavioral interventions and supports on student outcomes: A meta-analysis. *Journal of Positive Behavior Interventions, 23*(4), 235–251. https://doi.org/10.1177/1098300720952962
- Explores how PBIS, an integral part of behavioral MTSS, improves student outcomes and school climate.
22. Horner, R. H., Sugai, G., & Anderson, C. M. (2019). Examining the evidence base for school-wide positive behavioral interventions and supports. *Exceptional Children, 85*(2), 134–146. https://doi.org/10.1177/0014402918782618
- Reviews research supporting PBIS as a Tier 1 behavior intervention in MTSS.
23. Simonsen, B., Myers, D. M., & DeLuca, C. (2022). *Classroom behavior management: A multi-tiered approach to supporting student learning.* Guilford Press.
- Provides evidence-based strategies for integrating behavioral supports within Tier 1, 2, and 3 interventions.

2. Social-Emotional Learning (SEL) and Trauma-Informed MTSS

24. Osher, D., Kidron, Y., Brackett, M., Dymnicki, A., Jones, S., & Weissberg, R. P. (2020). Advancing the science and practice of social and emotional learning: Looking back and moving forward. *Review of Research in Education, 44*(1), 1–27. https://doi.org/10.3102/0091732X20903332

- Reviews research on the role of SEL in MTSS, with strategies for Tier 1 and Tier 2 social-emotional supports.
25. Darling-Churchill, K. E., & Lippman, L. (2021). Early childhood social and emotional development: Advancing the field of measurement. *Journal of Applied Developmental Psychology, 73*, 101215. https://doi.org/10.1016/j.appdev.2021.101215
- Discusses how SEL interventions within MTSS support students' early childhood development.
26. Blaustein, M. E., & Kinniburgh, K. M. (2018). *Treating traumatic stress in children and adolescents: How to foster resilience through attachment, self-regulation, and competency.* Guilford Press.
- Provides an MTSS-aligned framework for implementing trauma-informed interventions in schools.

Technology-Enhanced Professional Development (PD) for MTSS

3. Online and Hybrid Learning Models for Educator PD

27. Fishman, B. J., Dede, C., & Means, B. (2020). Teaching and technology: New tools for new times. *Review of Research in Education, 44*(1), 1–36. https://doi.org/10.3102/0091732X20902807
- Examines how technology can enhance asynchronous and hybrid PD models for MTSS training.
28. Darling-Hammond, L., Flook, L., Cook-Harvey, C., Barron, B., & Osher, D. (2019). Implications for educational practice of the science of learning and development. *Applied Developmental Science, 24*(2), 97–140. https://doi.org/10.1080/10888691.2018.1537791
- Explores online and blended learning approaches to professional development, including applications for MTSS.
29. Powell, S., & Bodur, Y. (2021). Professional development for inclusive education: Effective digital tools and strategies. *Journal of Special Education Technology, 36*(4), 263–278. https://doi.org/10.1177/01626434211000198
- Reviews digital PD tools, such as virtual coaching and interactive learning platforms, to support MTSS implementation.

4. Virtual Coaching and Data Systems for MTSS

30. Rock, M. L., Zigmond, N., Gregg, M., & Gable, R. A. (2021). Virtual coaching for teachers: A digital professional development model for improving MTSS fidelity. *Journal of Educational Psychology, 113*(2), 231–245. https://doi.org/10.1037/edu0000478
- Evaluates virtual coaching models and their impact on MTSS professional learning and intervention fidelity.

31. Mandinach, E. B., & Gummer, E. S. (2016). *Data literacy for educators: Making it count in teacher preparation and practice.* Teachers College Press.
   - Discusses how technology-based data systems help educators monitor student progress and refine MTSS interventions.

MTSS and Special Education

5. MTSS for Students with Disabilities and Inclusive Practices

32. O'Connor, R. E., Bocian, K. M., Beach, K. D., Sanchez, V., & Flynn, L. J. (2019). Special education and RTI: The role of instructionally valid assessments and evidence-based interventions. *Exceptional Children, 85*(1), 71–84. https://doi.org/10.1177/0014402918782618
   - Examines how MTSS interventions support students with disabilities and prevent unnecessary special education referrals.
33. McLeskey, J., Maheady, L., Billingsley, B. S., Brownell, M. T., & Lewis, T. J. (2022). *High-leverage practices for inclusive classrooms.* Routledge.
   - Provides **inclusive instructional strategies** for Tier 1 and Tier 2 MTSS interventions.
34. Cook, B. G., Tankersley, M., & Landrum, T. J. (2020). Special education and MTSS: Lessons from research and practice. *Remedial and Special Education, 41*(3), 133–146. https://doi.org/10.1177/0741932519832586
   - Reviews **MTSS as a framework for supporting special education students**, with a focus on individualized instruction.

6. Equity-Focused Special Education and MTSS

35. Losen, D. J., Hodson, C. L., Keith, M. A., Morrison, K., & Belway, S. (2017). *Disabling punishment: The need for remedies to the disparate loss of instructional time in special education.* UCLA Civil Rights Project.
   - Discusses how MTSS implementation can reduce disproportionality in special education referrals and disciplinary actions.
36. Sullivan, A. L., & Artiles, A. J. (2018). The promise and limitations of MTSS for achieving equity: Examining disparities in special education referrals. *Educational Researcher, 47*(7), 424–432. https://doi.org/10.3102/0013189X18796378
   - Highlights equity considerations in MTSS for students from diverse backgrounds and those with disabilities.

Conclusion

- ✓ These additional references provide a deeper exploration of key areas within MTSS professional development, including:
- ✓ Behavioral and social-emotional interventions (PBIS, SEL, trauma-informed care).
- ✓ Technology-enhanced professional learning models (virtual coaching, online PD).
- ✓ Special education and inclusive MTSS strategies.
- ✓ Equity-driven approaches to prevent disproportionality in special education referrals.

www.ingramcontent.com/pod-product-compliance
Lightning Source LLC
Chambersburg PA
CBHW081358290426
44110CB00018B/2406